Tax Guide 305

YOUR TRUSTEE DUTIES

by

Holmes F. Crouch
Tax Specialist

Published by

Allyear Tax Guides

**20484 Glen Brae Drive
Saratoga, CA 95070**

ISBN 0-944817-71-8

LCCN 2004108244

Printed in U.S.A.

Series 300
Retirees & Estates

Tax Guide 305

YOUR TRUSTEE DUTIES

[2nd Edition]

For other titles in print, see page 224.

The author: **Holmes F. Crouch**
For more about the author, see page 221.

PREFACE

If you are a knowledge-seeking **taxpayer** looking for information, this book can be helpful to you. It is designed to be read — from cover to cover — in about eight hours. Or, it can be "skim-read" in about 30 minutes.

Either way, you are treated to **tax knowledge** . . . *beyond the ordinary*. The "beyond" is that which cannot be found in IRS publications, the IRS web site, IRS e-file instructions, or tax software programs.

Taxpayers have different levels of interest in a selected subject. For this reason, this book starts with introductory fundamentals and progresses onward. You can verify the progression by chapter and section in the table of contents. In the text, "applicable law" is quoted in pertinent part. Key phrases and key tax forms are emphasized. Real-life examples are given . . . in down-to-earth style.

This book has 12 chapters. This number provides depth without cross-subject rambling. Each chapter starts with a head summary of meaningful information.

To aid in your skim-reading, informative diagrams and tables are placed strategically throughout the text. By leafing through page by page, reading the summaries and section headings, and glancing at the diagrams and tables, you can get a good handle on the matters covered.

Effort has been made to update and incorporate all of the latest tax law changes that are *significant* to the title subject. However, "beyond the ordinary" does not encompass every conceivable variant of fact and law that might give rise to protracted dispute and litigation. Consequently, if a particular statement or paragraph is crucial to your own specific case, you are urged to seek professional counseling. Otherwise, the information presented is general and is designed for a broad range of reader interests.

The Author

INTRODUCTION

Undeniably, there are magic and aura in the word "trust." There is mysticism also. There is a spiritual belief that once a trust is created and a trustee appointed, all earthly duties of managing and distributing trust property are achieved through celestial communion and surrealism. Thereafter, a trust is self-perpetuating . . . and nonaccountable. Any person who suggests otherwise is deemed an adversary to the wonders of cyberspace.

Dream on — all you trustors, trustees, and beneficiaries of a trust. There's a whole world of reality out there.

A trust is a separate legal entity of its own. It is a creation of Man: not of God. It is created under state law which imposes duties and responsibilities on all of the parties thereto. It is administered under federal law where onerous tasks of taxation and accountability are imposed.

A trust is NOT an avoidance vehicle. Yes, in some living trust cases, probate may be avoided or at least minimized. Taxes, however, cannot be avoided, though in some cases they may be "diluted." Nor can a trust avoid the repayment of debts and satisfaction of liabilities by the trustor. In the most succinct terms possible, a trust — primarily and foremost — is a **property distribution vehicle**. If you assimilate this one concept alone, you have come a long way in understanding how trusts work.

A "trustor," by the way, is a living individual who formulates a trust contract. A "trustee" is an appointee of the trustor to manage and distribute the trust property. A "beneficiary" is the recipient of trust property, or the income from it, in accordance with the distributive terms of the trust contract.

There is marketing magic in the various terms used to describe a particular trust arrangement. Most family and personal trusts are promotionally described as—

Pure trusts, constitutional trusts, by-pass trusts, tax-free trusts, marital deduction trusts, spendthrift trusts, generation-skipping trusts, charitable remainder trusts, estate planning trusts, split-interest trusts, private foundation trusts, . . . etc. etc.

In this book, all of these and similar descriptive variants are treated as *gratuitous trusts*. They are "gratuitous" in the sense that no beneficiary is obligated to make payment to, perform services for, or give a reciprocal promise to the trustor or trustee of such trust. Where a trustor is a trustee, and also a beneficiary, watch out! Such arrangements merge into the high-flying realm of sham and grantor trusts. High-flyer trusts are **not** what this book is all about.

Our focus is strictly down to earth. A trustor with distributive assets of substantial value wants to distribute his/her assets to one or more beneficiaries over a period of time, usually more than one year. The trustor, however, has no intention of doing so until after he/she dies. When the trustor dies, the trustee "takes over" to do what the trustor cannot himself/herself do in afterlife. Therefore, we have a lot to tell you about the duties of a trustee.

Firstly, we want to discount the various myths associated with trusts, and explain how trusts are supposed to work (after a trustor's death). We'll also cite specific legal duties expected of you under state law where the trust contract was prepared. We'll provide guidance on dissecting the contract — some 35 pages or so of legalese — and on getting down to the business of rearranging and managing the trust property.

We also have to tell you about the sources of trust income that you must track, and your obligation to file **Form 1041**: *U.S. Income Tax Return for Trusts*, whenever said income reaches or exceeds $600 in a given year. When you distribute non-exempt income to a beneficiary, there is **Schedule K-1**: *Beneficiary's Share of Income, Deductions, Credits, etc.* to be prepared. In addition, there are property transactions reportings to be made, recordkeeping chores to attend to, and procedures to follow when terminating the trust. Eventually, all trusts must terminate.

Although the thrust of this book is trustee driven, the information presented is also vital to trustors (who appoint the initial and successor trustees). Furthermore, the information is helpful to beneficiaries who must look to the trustee for accountability and due diligence in the management of trust property. The more knowledgeable all parties are regarding the activities of a trust, the more satisfying the experience will be.

CONTENTS

Chapter   **Page**

1. OVERCOMING THE MYTHS................   **1-1**

The "Revocability" Myth.............................   1- 2
The "Exhibit A" Myth................................   1- 3
The "No Probate" Myth.............................   1- 5
Property Titling Awkwardness....................   1- 7
The "Outstate" Myth.................................   1- 8
The "No Hassle" Myth..............................   1- 9
The "Pure Privacy" Myth   1-11
The "QTIP Trust" Myth   1-12
The "No Waiting Time" Myth....................   1-14

2. HOW TRUSTS REALLY WORK..........   **2-1**

Like a "Bonded Warehouse" 2- 2
Role & Qualifications of Trustor................   2- 5
Limitations on Trust Property....................   2- 6
Preferred Types of Property 2- 8
Trustee Qualifications...............................   2- 9
Trust Instrument: General Contents............   2-11
Meaning of "Power of Appointment"   2-13
How Trustees Are Weakened....................   2-15
Check Your Trust Law.............................   2-16
Uneconomical Trusts................................   2-18

3. LEGAL DUTIES OF TRUSTEE **3-1**

Beware of Covetous Attorneys...................   3- 2
Compact Edition of Trust Law..................   3- 3
Digest of Prescribed Duties.......................   3- 5
Avoid Conflicts of Interest 3- 7
The "Prudent Person" Standard..................   3- 8
Many Trustee Powers...............................   3-10
Specific Statutory Powers.........................   3-11
Compensation for Services........................   3-13
Breach of Trust Actions............................   3-15

Chapter	Page

4. DISSECTING THE CONTRACT **4-1**

Photocopy the Original 4- 2
Prepare Table of Contents 4- 3
Clarify Name of Trust 4- 4
Article I: Example Styles 4- 6
Disregard During-Life Provisions 4- 8
The After-Death Paragraphs 4-10
Scope the Trust Estate 4-12
Any Generational Skips? 4-14
Enshrine Your Powers 4-15

5. GETTING DOWN TO BUSINESS **5-1**

Verify Payment of Transfer Taxes 5- 2
Apply for Trust Tax ID 5- 4
Open Checking-Only Account 5- 5
Collect All Monetary Assets 5- 6
Open Investment Account 5- 8
Plan Property Rearrangement 5- 9
Register Beneficiaries & Preferences 5-11
Dispose of Outstate Property 5-14
Stabilize Your Modus Operandi 5-17
Set Up Books of Account 5-19

6. INTRODUCTION TO FORM 1041 .... **6-1**

Head Portion of Form 1041 .... 6- 2
Type of Entity Checkboxes 6- 4
Simple vs. Complex Trusts 6- 6
General Format, Page 1 .... 6- 7
Income Distribution Deduction 6- 9
Exemption Amounts Compared 6-11
Tax Rate Bands Compared 6-12
What If There's Loss? 6-13
More Checkboxes & Questions 6-14
Any Wages Assigned? 6-16
Foreign Accounts & Trusts 6-17

7.   SOURCES OF TRUST INCOME   7-1

There Are 8 Sources 7- 2
Interest & Dividend Income 7- 3
Use Schedule B: Form 1040 .... 7- 5
Directly Owned Real Estate 7- 6
Indirectly Owned Real Estate, Etc. 7- 8
Transactional Gains & Losses 7- 9
Business & Farm Income 7-11
Three "Heavy Hitters" 7-13
Nontaxable Income 7-14

8.   ADMINISTRATIVE DEDUCTIONS   8-1

Overview of Deductions 8- 2
Interest Paid on Trust Debt 8- 3
Deductible Taxes Limited 8- 5
Fiduciary Fees 8- 6
Charitable Contributions 8- 7
Applicability of Schedule A (1041) 8- 9
Legal & Accounting Fees 8-11
Other Deductions Not Subject 8-12
Determining the 2% Floor 8-14
Expenses Affected by 2% Floor 8-16
Adjusted Total Income 8-17

9.   THE DISTRIBUTION DEDUCTION   9-1

Simple Trust Defined 9- 2
Section 661: Complex Trusts 9- 4
Character of Amounts Distributed 9- 5
Limitation on Deduction 9- 7
DNI Computational Sequence 9- 8
Adjusted Tax-Exempt Income 9-10
Capital Gains & Losses 9-11
The Capital Inclusion Steps 9-12
If DNI Zero: Stop 9-15
Continuation Beyond DNI 9-15

Chapter	Page

10. THE BENEFICIARY K-1s 10-1

The Start-off Instructions............................	10- 2
Section 652: Simple Trusts........................	10- 4
Section 662: Complex Trusts	10- 5
K-1 Income Assignments	10- 7
Characterizing K-1 Income........................	10- 9
Material Participation: The Key	10-10
Deductions & Credits Limited....................	10-11
A Simple Trust Example...........................	10-13
Other Simple K-1 Uses.............................	10-15
Complex Trusts & Charities......................	10-17

11. TAX AND PAYMENTS 11-1

Taxable Income Revisited..........................	11- 2
Overview of Schedule G	11- 4
Capital Gains Example..............................	11- 6
Alternative Minimum Tax	11- 7
Foreign Tax Credit....................................	11- 9
Household Employment Tax	11-11
Accumulations for Charities......................	11-12
Payments with Extensions	11-13
Estimated Payment Vouchers	11-15

12. TERMINATING THE TRUST 12-1

Identify "The Event"..................................	12- 2
What Probate Law Says	12- 4
What the IRS Says	12- 6
Notify the Beneficiaries	12- 7
Accounting for Liquidation Proceeds	12- 9
The "Final Year Loss" Rule.......................	12-11
Excerpts from Regulations........................	12-12
The Final K-1	12-14
The Final 1041...	12-17
Keep a Contingency Reserve	12-19

1

OVERCOMING THE MYTHS

Living Trusts, A Highly Popular Form Of "Estate Planning," Are Clouded With Myths And Misconceptions. Avoidance Of Probate Is Possible And This Translates, By Association, Into Avoidance Of Creditors, Taxes, And Other Disclosures. With Marital Trusts, The BIG SURPRISE To The Surviving Trustor Is The "QTIP Myth." Property Titling Is Always Awkward In A Trust, Especially With Outstate And Foreign Holdings. If "Exhibit A" Is Incomplete Or Inaccurate, There Is Misinterpretation Of What Property Is Actually In The Trust. When A Trustor Dies, There Is A "Suspension Period" Of From 6 To 18 Months.

For most persons, there is an aura about family trusts. They are viewed as celestial arrangements for the assignment of assets where privacy rules supreme, and where the assets are beyond the reach of the tax and legal systems of the day. Once a trust is created on paper, it is believed, everything is taken care of in life . . . and in afterlife. It is the perfect estate plan: self-administering, self-distributing, and self-terminating (when the time is ripe). Consequently, trusts are often portrayed as the true magic wand for entry through the Pearly Gates.

The truth is: trusts are not magic. They are loaded with tax traps, accounting traps, probate traps, property titling traps, privacy traps, and irritation traps. They require expert legal setup, continuous management, annual accounting, and periodic legal defenses. They are **not** the path to utopia.

One of the major misconceptions concerning trusts has to do with *transfer tax* matters: gift tax, death tax, and/or generation-skipping transfer tax. These taxes — federal and state (where applicable) — must be determined and paid, before the trust property is "released" to the trustee. Usually, an **executor** is appointed for transfer accounting purposes. It is for this reason that the duties of an executor differ markedly from those of a trustee.

In this introductory chapter, therefore, we want to identify the common myths associated with family and personal trusts. We want to do this in an informative and instructional way that will cause you not to be misled by them. Our position is that, if you know what the myths are, you are less subject to bewilderment by reality and more likely to appreciate the true benefits of a trust. As a designated trustee (or a trustor who has appointed, or is about to appoint, a trustee), you particularly want to try hard to overcome any popular misconceptions you may have concerning trusts. Otherwise, you will find it difficult to settle down to the serious business of prescribing and managing trust property.

The "Revocability" Myth

By far, the great majority of family trusts these days originate from the formulation of *Living Trusts*. These are documents prepared during a trustor's life, transferring his living powers over his property to a trustee , which powers take effect after the death of the trustor. A "trustor" is the creator or originator of a trust. A "trustee" is the manager of the trustor's property, after the trustor's death.

During the life of a trustor, he can assign property and other assets to his trust. He can amend the terms of the trust after the assignment. He can exchange his properties and assets, or can replace them with other property and other assets. Or, he can withdraw all property from the trust and revoke the trust contract altogether. He can do whatever he wants with his property and assets . . . so long as he is alive.

Because of the revocability feature of a living trust, the myth evolves that one can only do this with a trust. This simply is not true. The power to revoke a living trust contract and/or its assigned assets has nothing whatsoever to do — nor is it exclusive — with the creation of a trust. We'll repeat this. The right of a trustor to assign, reassign, or revoke his assignment(s) altogether has nothing to do with the creation of a trust.

One has a similar right when preparing a will. One also has a similar right when preparing any kind of contract which is not a trust. Furthermore, one has a similar right with a blank piece of paper. On a piece of paper, one can list selected assets; he can change them around; or he can erase them from the paper altogether. Similarly, one can draw a box in the sand. He can place in the box various objects representing his property holdings; he can rearrange them; he can demolish some (representing consumption); he can leave in the box whatever remains, or he can take them all out.

What we are telling you is this: The right of revocation — changing, substituting, amending, withdrawing — of one's property in trust is not an inherent special feature of a living trust. A trustor has no additional rights with respect to his property holdings than he would have *without* a trust. Property rights are inherent to the owner of property (while living). They are not inherent to the character of a trust contract. Property rights are **fundamental to mankind**. They are not fundamental to a piece of paper, no matter how prestigious the legal technicians are who prepared the trust instrument. We urge that you keep this fundamental point in mind at all times.

The "Exhibit A" Myth

Most living trust documents are quite voluminous. They don't need to be, but they are. They range from 25 to 50 pages, averaging about 35 pages per contract. All end with a single — what we call *Exhibit A* paragraph. The Exhibit A is where all the property disclosures and transfers are made.

The typical Exhibit A paragraph reads as follows:

*The Trustors hereby grant and assign the property listed on the attached **Exhibit A** to the Trustee, and the Trustee hereby acknowledges acceptance of the property IN TRUST upon the terms and conditions herein stated.*

IN WITNESS WHEREOF, the Trustor(s) and Trustee(s) have executed this Agreement on this _____ day of ___(month)___, ___(year)___.

/s/_____   /s/_____
JOHN J. JONES, Trustor   *JOHN J. JONES, Trustee*

/s/_____   /s/_____
MARY M. JONES, Trustor   *MARY M. JONES, Trustee*

(These names are entirely fictitious.) The trustor and trustee signatures are witnessed by a Notary Public who, more often than not, is the attorney who prepared the trust agreement.

Typically, after the trust agreement is signed, the preparer informs the trustor that Exhibit A is a requirement of state law. That is, it is a necessary document of its own for "funding the trust." The property items listed on Exhibit A, when titled in the name of the trust, transform the words and paragraphs of the agreement into a viable legal entity which becomes operative upon death of the trustor. Otherwise, without at least some property listed on Exhibit A, the trust is a nonentity.

What frequently happens is that, when the trust preparer explains the importance of Exhibit A, the trustor nods his head, signifying his understanding of the situation. The preparer then offers to do the property titling documentation. Since the trustor hasn't thought the matter through, he further signifies that he will decide later on which properties and assets to assign to his trust. Thus the myth arises that Exhibit A is "all taken care of." In reality, the opposite is true.

In the great majority of living trust creations, Exhibit A is rarely ever completed. Even when legally initiated with the listing of a token asset thereon, there is seldom any meaningful follow-through. As a trustee, therefore, your duty is **not** to assume that Exhibit A is funded and operative. Instead, insist on examining Exhibit A while the trustor is alive. If warranted, and with permission of the trustor, re-engage the trust preparer and pay whatever professional fees are required to do Exhibit A right. Because of different property interests and wishes of trustors, the preparation of a completed Exhibit A is not automatically included in the preparation of the living trust contract. As depicted in Figure 1.1, the Trust Agreement and Exhibit A, though related, are entirely two different preparatory matters.

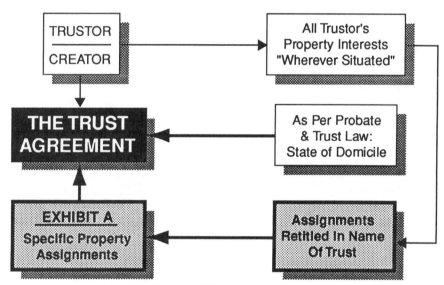

Fig. 1.1 - The Essential Documents of a Living Trust

The "No, Probate" Myth

The promoters of living trusts masterfully assert that such trusts avoid probate and, therefore, avoid probate fees and probate time. There is — or could be — some truth in this. But the avoidance of probate is not automatic, nor is it guaranteed. Probate avoidance pertains only to that property which has been retitled in the name of the trust at or before the trustor's death. Let us explain.

The term "probate" has acquired an ugly and sinister name. It engenders wild visions of painful, punitive, and irreconcilable entanglements in a corrupt legal system designed to fatten the pockets of attorneys at the expense of one's heirs and legatees. Attorneys themselves are much to blame for this widely held view. In some states, and in some courts, the probate process can become protracted, costly, and unsatisfying. As a result, any hint of an opportunity to avoid probate is jumped at by the uninformed.

Avoidance of probate requires that title to property be held in a form **other than** the individual name of the owner thereof. One avoidance form is joint tenancy with right of survivorship. Another form is by gifting or quitclaiming the property to others *before* the owner's death. Still another form is to transfer property into a trust prior to one's death. This is the power and merit of a living trust. Property can be assigned and titled thereto *before* the death of a trustor. If it is, property which is in the trust at time of death does indeed avoid probate.

As a trustee, if you understand this concept, you will be many steps ahead of your contemporaries. To help you visualize the probate avoidance concept, we present Figure 1.2. Particularly note our emphasis on BEFORE DEATH. Whatever is listed on Exhibit A before death, and clearly titled in the name of the trust, avoids probate. If there is no Exhibit A, there is no probate avoidance. It is just that simple. If there is only a partial Exhibit A, there is only partial probate avoidance.

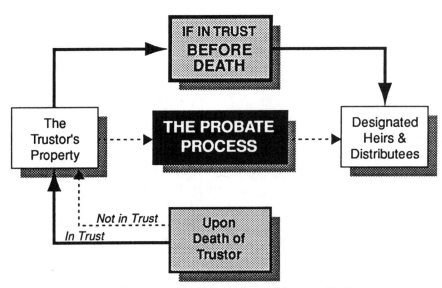

Fig. 1.2 - The Concept of Probate Avoidance with Trusts

Property Titling Awkwardness

Having property in a living trust before one's death can cause awkward titling problems. If trust property is not titled correctly under the laws of the state where the property is situated or where the trustee is domiciled, legal entanglements and challenges can arise. The entanglements become most aggravating when the property is sold, exchanged, or "switched around" among various trustors, trustees, and new owners. An example or two may illustrate our point.

Suppose a trustor's name is John J. Jones (our previous fictitious trustor). He establishes a trust called: THE JOHN J. JONES TRUST. As the trustor, he is the initial trustee thereof. He drew up and formalized his trust agreement on July 17, 2004. He owns a parcel of land out in the foothills on which he hopes to build his dream home someday. How does he title that parcel of land which he has now assigned to his trust?

The simplest form of titling would be—

The John J. Jones Trust
UDT July 17, 2004
John J Jones, Trustee

The letters "UDT" stand for: "Under Declaration of Trust." Also used are the letters "UTA" (Under Trust Agreement), "DTD" (Declaration of Trust Dated), and other similar abbreviations. These letters refer to the underlying trust instrument which must precede the titling process.

Suppose, after a few years Jones decides to sell or exchange his parcel of land for another parcel more to his liking. Will the title company, realtor, or attorney representing the buyer or exchanger want to become involved in the legal uncertainties of the trust instrument? Most probably not. The buyer or exchanger certainly doesn't want his property clouded with the trustor's intentions. In most cases, the legal representative of the buyer/exchanger will insist that the trustor remove the property from the trust, retitle it in his personal name, then grant deed it to the personal name of the buyer or the exchanger. It is always preferable to deal with a living human being than with a fictitious entity.

If the trustor is married, and he and his spouse have a joint and survivors trust arrangement, property titling and transferring can become quite cumbersome. For example, the property in trust might be titled as—

The Jones Family Trust
UDT July 17, 2004
John Jones, Trustee, or Mary Jones, Trustee,
or their successor trustees

Can you not imagine the legal, accounting, and computer input problems that can arise when transferring electronically three different mutual funds A, B, and C in the trust to three new investment accounts D, E, and F that Jones also wants in his trust?

As a trustor or trustee, ask yourself these questions: Would you want to acquire property titled in someone else's trust? Or, would you prefer to acquire the property from a living human being? If you would prefer dealing with a living human, why would someone else prefer to deal with *your* (inhuman) trust entity? For engaging in entrepreneurial activities while you are living, the whole trust titling process is awkward and unwieldy.

The "Outstate" Myth

Each of the 50 U.S. states has its own probate and trust law. Accordingly, each state asserts absolute sovereignty over all persons and property domiciled within its borders. If a trustor lives in one state, has property in a second state, and a designated trustee in a third state, three separate state trust laws are involved. For this situation, ideally, three separate trust instruments would have to be prepared: one for each jurisdiction.

The promoters of living trusts assume the position that having persons and property in different states is no problem. "All states recognize trust instruments," they say. As a broad generality, this is true. It is from generalities like this that myths about trusts emerge. The unshaken belief grows that a trustor who creates a trust in one state will have his trust intentions recognized in any other state where his appointees and property may be. This belief is deceptive.

True, all states recognize trusts . . . but only when prepared under their own probate and trust law. A trustor domiciled in California, for example, who has rental real estate in Texas, and a pleasure boat in Florida, cannot expect Texas and Florida to accept his California trust carte blanche. Upon death of the trustor and the presentation of credentials by the trustee, Texas and Florida each will insist on probate-like proceedings with respect to any and all of the trustor's real and tangible property within their state borders. There are exceptions for intangible assets such as bank accounts, mutual funds, stocks and bonds, and insurance policies.

To increase the jurisdictional complexity a bit, suppose you, the designated trustee, are domiciled in the state of Colorado. After the trustor is deceased and his estate settled (that is, all designated property transferred into the trust), the trust assets then come under the jurisdiction of Colorado. All states treat the domicile of the trustee (after the trustor's death) as the administrative situs of the trust property.

Still worse are the jurisdictional problems when a trustor has real property outside of the U.S. For example, a vacation condo in Spain, land in Argentina, and an office building in the Philippines. The property titling awkwardness exampled earlier becomes a holy mess. We try to dramatize the situation for you in Figure 1.3.

Our message is that, as a trustee, you should be aware of all real or tangible property located in a different state — or different country — from that of the domicile of the trustor.

The "No Hassle" Myth

Trusts are often portrayed as legal entities which "take care of themselves." Because the trust may avoid some probate features, you are told that there are no problems and no hassles when administering trust property. You are instructed that, once a trust is set up and title to its assets becomes irrevocable, you as trustee can distribute its income and assets promptly and expeditiously. There is "no hassle," you may be told.

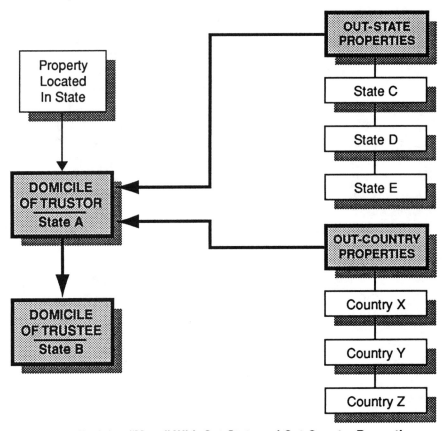

Fig. 1.3 - Retitling "Mess" With Out-State and Out-Country Properties

The truth is that trusts are NOT self-administering. They are not free of hassles. Nor are they free of the pesky problems of management, accounting, and adequate security. If anything, there are more legal constraints on trusts than there are on human beings.

Technically, when a trustor dies, that property which is already in trust may begin to be distributed at any time. But, what if the trustor owes debts, owes taxes, has mortgages on the property, has liens on the assets, and so on? All valid debts, taxes, mortgages, and liens have to be satisfied (discharged) before the trust property is free and clear. If the income and assets of the trust are distributed prematurely, who pays for the outstanding debts and taxes?

Answer: If trust property is distributed imprudently or prematurely, the **trustee** himself (or herself) has to pay the unsatisfied debts and taxes out of his own pocket . . . unless.   That is, unless he can persuade the distributees to return to the trust a pro rata share of the money that they have already received.   Most distributees treat trust money as free gifts from heaven.   Not only would they refuse to return any money, they would threaten to sue the trustee for misconduct and negligence.   Fortunately, most trust instruments try to protect the trustee against such lawsuits, provided he acts prudently and in good faith.

The net result is that trustees are no more free of everyday business, personal, and legal hassles than are other managers of property.   As long as a trust is irrevocable and in operation, the hassles are ongoing.   There are hassles with attorneys, with accountants, with regulatory agencies, with tax agencies, with creditors, with computers, with distributees, and with anyone else — person or entity — who claims an interest in the trust property.

The "Pure Privacy" Myth

In the early days of U.S. history — prior to 1936 particularly — trusts were a popular means of defrauding creditors and tax collectors.   Property, once transferred (irrevocably) into a trust was out of reach of the probing eyes of creditors, promoters, legal technicians, tax collectors, and government agencies.   This led to the myth that trusts are the ultimate in pure privacy when conducting one's financial affairs.

No more!

Today, with our legal system so sharply honed, tax collection so mandatory, and government so pervasive, trusts offer only a modicum of privacy in property affairs.   This modicum is no greater and no less than that which an ordinary citizen enjoys in private property rights.   Bluntly stated, personal trusts cannot be used to avoid the valid debts, taxes, or liens against the trustor(s).

Still, the privacy myth prevails.   This arises largely from the fact that, when an individual dies, notice of his/her death is published locally in a newspaper of general circulation.   If a trust is in existence at the time, only a notice in the obituary section is required.

If there is no trust, a formal Notice of Death and Petition to Administer Estate is required. This legal notice "invites" all heirs, beneficiaries, creditors, contingent creditors, and those persons or entities who may be interested in the property of the decedent, to come forth and stake a valid claim. In other words, without a trust, the property of a decedent is exposed to the public domain through probate filings and public records.

There is one privacy protection that trusts do offer. If the trustees, heirs, and beneficiaries of the trust property themselves owe debts, taxes, and mortgages, the trust property is indeed protected. So long as the trustor (or his estate) has paid off his own debts and obligations, the trust property is not subject to any claim or hypothecation by the designated distributees of that property. That is, any debt of a distributee is not collectible until that distributee's share of the property or income is actually transferred out of the trust, in accordance with the terms of the trust instrument. This is called the "spendthrift protection" aspect of a trust. We depict this concept for you in Figure 1.4. Otherwise, trusts offer no particular privacy protection that cannot be achieved by other means.

The "QTIP Trust" Myth

In the case of married trustors (husband and wife, both living), an ingenious myth is perpetuated by the promoters of family living trusts. The myth is wrapped up in the acronym: *QTIP Trust* (Qualified Terminable Interest Property). This QTIP thing is more popularly referred to as a Marital Deduction Trust, or "marital trust" for short. Its origin stems from Section 2056(a) of the Internal Revenue Code: *Bequests to Surviving Spouse; Allowance of Marital Deduction.*

In essence, Section 2056(a) allows a quite substantial marital deduction against the taxable estate of a decedent trustor. Depending on a trustor's other prearrangements for his surviving spouse, the amount of marital deduction can be so substantial that it alone virtually eliminates any death tax to the first decedent trustor. Achieving this desirable result necessitates the separate designation of a "qualified terminable interest property" [IRC Sec. 2056(b)(7)(B)]. Trust promoters pounce on this special deduction

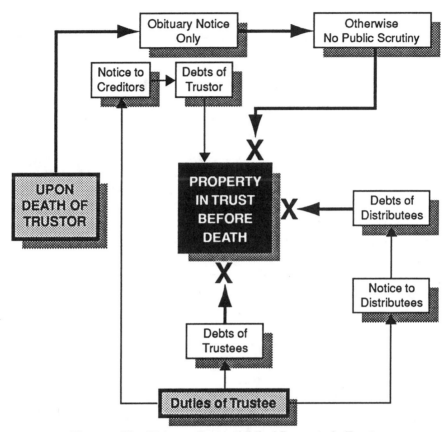

Fig. 1.4 - The "Privacy Protection" of Property in Trust

to write into the trust instrument the establishment of a QTIP trust upon death of the first decedent trustor. This immediately triggers the necessity for **two** separate trusts: the survivor's trust and the marital trust. Complexity and obfuscation mount.

The effect of the marital (QTIP) trust is that the surviving spouse is entitled to all income from the QTIP property for life. In addition, the survivor has the right to invade the QTIP corpus for whatever funds are needed for *an ascertainable standard of support, maintenance, and health.* This is about as much information that the trustors ever know about the so-called marital trust. They are left with the impression that any QTIP property remaining at time of death of the surviving trustor is free of any subsequent death tax. This positively is not so. Furthermore, a surviving spouse, whether a trustor or not, has identically the same rights to marital deduction property.

Trust promoters/preparers fail to inform husband-wife trustors that any and all residual QTIP property is mandatorily included in the gross estate of the surviving trustor. In other words, being a qualified deduction against the first decedent trustor's estate, it must be included in the second decedent trustor's estate. This re-inclusion mandate is the very feature that qualifies the QTIP as a deduction in the first instance. It is a tentative deduction only; it is not an outright exemption. We sometimes feel that this omission of material information is intentional. After all, when both trustors are deceased, it is up to the trustee to figure out what to do. If he missteps in any way, litigious onlookers start their inroads into the residual estate.

Section 2044 of the IR Code makes this re-inclusion point clear. Said section is titled: ***Certain Property for Which Marital Deduction was Previously Allowed.*** It reads in part—

> *The value of the gross estate shall include the value of any property . . . in which the decedent had a qualifying income interest for life . . . by reason of section 2056(b)(7).*

We're curious. How many attorneys, legal technicians, and trust preparers have discussed this QTIP re-inclusion requirement with you (either as trustor or trustee)? Our bet is: few if any.

The "No Waiting Time" Myth

In our view, trust promoters engender a common cardinal sin. They create the impression that, with a living trust, there is no waiting time between the death of a trustor and the takeover by his trustee. This is just not so. Legally, perhaps, the point is arguable if the executor and trustee are one and the same person. Even so, a domain of time is required for making the necessary property appraisals, accountings, assignments, and transitions from a decedent's estate to his trust estate.

When a U.S. citizen or U.S. resident dies, all property transfers to his successors, including those assigned to a trust, are *suspended . . . temporarily*. This suspension is required by "operation of law": both State and Federal. The purpose of suspension is to allow adequate time for *settling the estate* of the decedent before full trust operations begin. In other words, as depicted in Figure 1.5, it takes a certain amount of finite time to wrap up all the affairs of a decedent before a new chapter of property management begins. The more complex the estate affairs, the longer the suspension period required.

What are the decedent's affairs to be wrapped up and settled?

There are *five* categories of such activities, namely:

1. Notification of decedent's creditors and confirmation of amounts outstanding; most state laws require at least four months for this legal notification process.

2. Inventory and appraisal of all the decedent's assets: real, tangible, and intangible; typically at least six months are required for this, IF all real and tangible assets are physically within the state of domicile of the decedent.

3. If real estate or tangible property items are located out-state or out-country, contact must be made with administrative authorities and legal counselors therein; in the best of circumstances, it takes at least a year to settle nondomiciliary matters.

4. Preparation and filing of federal death tax return and state inheritance tax return when gross estate exceeds $1,500,000; nine months from date of death is the statutory time for filing, though a 6-month extension can be obtained.

5. Notification of all heirs, beneficiaries, trustees, charities, and other distributees designated by the decedent, that the estate is about to be closed; a general description of the property, its appraised value, and the approximate amount of money to be distributed to each should be provided.

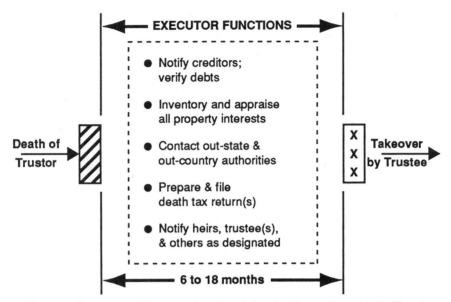

Fig. 1.5 - Necessary "Suspension Time" for Settling a Decedent's Estate

With respect to the federal death tax returns, Section 6018(a)(1): *Estate Tax Returns; Citizens or Residents*, says very specifically—

> *In all cases where the gross estate at the death of a citizen or resident exceeds the applicable exclusion amount in effect* [$1,000,000 to $2,000,000], *the executor shall make a return with respect to the estate tax imposed by* [Section 2001(c)].

The whole point we're trying to make is that there are important matters to be taken care of, before a trustee can take charge and take over. The death tax return and related business are performed by the **executor** of a decedent's estate: not by the trustee of his trust. Although the executor and trustee may be one and the same, (we advise against this), functionally — and timewise — the two sets of duties are quite different. If the same person "wears two hats," so to speak, errors and omissions mount and litigative issues rise. It is for this reason, among others, that the executor and trustee functions should be separated.

2

HOW TRUSTS REALLY WORK

A Trust Comprises A Trustor, Trust Property, Trustee, Trust Instrument, And One Or More Beneficiaries. The Property Conveyed Should Be Of Significant Value And Capable Of Generating INCOME And CAPITAL For Distributions Of Money To The Beneficiaries. Preferred Types Are Real Estate, Marketable Securities, Solvent Businesses, And Rare Collectibles. A General Power To "Appoint" Trust Property At Whim Is Dangerous, As Are Too Many Generational Distributees. A Trustee Should Be Over Age 35 And Not Intimidated By Attorneys. Also, He Should REVIEW TRUST LAW Of The State Where The Property Is Domiciled.

The underlying premise of this book is that you, as the reader, are either a trustor or trustee and that a trust instrument/document does indeed exist. The trust instrument was prepared either by a qualified attorney or other professional who has intimate knowlege of the Probate and Trust Law of the state of domicile of the trustor. We are not concerned here with the type of trust — be it personal, family, marital, alimony, child support, gift-to-minors, spendthrift, medical, educational, charitable, generation-skipping, etc. We are only concerned with the fact that it is irrevocable. Once a trust is irrevocable, the focus is on how the trust works, and what are its advantages and limitations.

Probably the best way to get a focus-handle on the workings of a trust is to think of it as a cross between a will and a corporation. A will has certain testamentary and operation-of-law features which a trust also has. A will, however, is limited to a one-time final distribution of the decedent's property. In contrast, a trust can engage in extended distributions of property over substantial periods of time . . . up to 25 to 50 years or so.

A corporation, we all know, engages in business activities which a trust also can engage in. One of the property holdings of a trust may itself be a corporation or some other business entity such as a partnership or proprietorship. The operational motivation of a corporation is totally entrepreneurial. It seeks to develop and expand into ever-widening markets and products. In contrast, the operational focus of a trust is on preservation of capital, continuous distribution of income, and, ultimately, termination of the trust. Whereas a trust has extended life, it is **not** indefinite. A corporation, however, has indefinite life. Both a trust and a corporation are creations of state law. They are not creations of God such as are trustors, trustees, and beneficiaries.

Accordingly, in this chapter we want to dwell on the bona fide characteristics of a working trust. In Chapter 1, we tried to dispel the mysticism and mystique of trusts. Now we want to discuss the features of a trust that really make it work. The fundamental key for doing so is the role of the trustee: his attention to business, his comprehension of property arrangements, his discretionary powers, and his ability to communicate with the beneficiaries of the trust. Always be mindful that, at some point downstream, the trust property must all be distributed and the trust terminated. The duties of a trustee then cease.

Like a "Bonded Warehouse"

The most practical way of dealing with a trust is to think of it as a warehouse for the storage of property. Once filled and irrevocable, it becomes a *bonded warehouse*. It is security bonded in the sense that it is "constructed" under state law, and the "manager-in-charge" (the trustee) has legal obligations and restraints imposed on him, also by state law. In addition, federal surety-type bonding applies in the form of *Grantor Trust Rules* [IRC Sections 671-679]. These rules forbid any "interested person" from entering the warehouse and removing any property for his own benefit.

As a bonded warehouse, what are the features of a trust that make it work and function for its intended purpose?

There are at least eight features — or primary components — which make a trust work. In synopsis form, these eight components are:

1. TRUSTOR — the creator of the trust and the transferor of designated property thereinto.

2. TRUST INSTRUMENT — the agreement, declaration, contract, or other legal document prepared in accordance with applicable state law.

3. TRUST LAW — the probate code of the state of domicile of the trustor **and** of the state of situs of out-state real and tangible property; trust law is identified by its own section in the probate code with such title words as: *Creation, Validity, Modification, and Termination of Trusts.*

4. TRUST PROPERTY — specific property assignments either predesignated by Exhibit A of a living trust, by irrevocable transfers while the trustor is alive, or by testamentary transfers in a will at time of the trustor's death. Once irrevocably assigned, the trust entity is the *legal owner* of the property therein.

5. TRUSTEE — the *manager* of the trust property pursuant to instructions to him enumerated in the trust instrument; as said manager, he is entitled to a trustee fee.

6. BENEFICIARIES — one or more living human beings and specified generational unborns of existing human beings; these persons are the *beneficial owners* of the trust property.

7. CHARITIES — qualified tax-exempt organizations specifically designated by will or the trust, or as selected by the trustee where such discretionary powers are granted by the trustor.

8. PROBATE COURT — the judicial process for resolving any disputes and claims by creditors, beneficiaries, state authorities, and charities; probate jurisdiction is limited to ownership matters, beneficial rights, and trustee malfeasance. Probate courts have no jurisdiction over federal tax matters.

As a summary of the above "working components" of a trust, we present Figure 2.1. Not all trusts provide for charities; there is no requirement that they do so provide. A charity can be thought of as a remainder beneficiary for clearing out the clutter of a trust and simplifying its administration: tax and nontax.

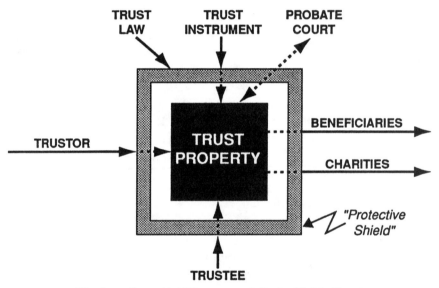

Fig. 2.1 - Essential "Components" of a Viable Trust

With Figure 2.1 as a reference guide, let us describe the features of a trust more definitively than we have given above. We want you to see a trust through the eyes of the IRS. Operationally, financially, and functionally, the IRS has more veto power over a trust than any state agency, including probate court. This IRS power exists because, in the final analysis, trusts **are** taxable entities. If not directly taxable, they are *tax accountable* every year.

Role & Qualifications of Trustor

A trustor, first off, has to be a human being. He has to own property of value that can be useful to others after his demise. Here, the term "property" means any form of assets: real, tangible, and intangible — whether owned in his own right, in co-ownership with others, or aggregated into an ongoing business which he controls. A trustor also has to have someone whom he can trust to manage and care for his property once it is irrevocably assigned to his trust. Regardless of trust law legalese, he is not required to put all of his property in trust. There is a lot of clutter in every human being's estate which is best left out of the trust.

The role of a trustor is defined more by the kind and value of property than by any other single factor. If he has property co-owned with others, his percentage of ownership interest must be clearly ascertainable in one or more evidentiary documents. By "property of value," we mean that which has *significant market value.* By "significant value," we mean property which is coveted by someone else to the point that the trustor would fight to protect his ownership interests. After all, if you put an old pair of shoes in a trust, who really cares? But if you put a parcel of waterfront land in trust, there would be many persons and entities in the public domain who would covet that property for their own uses.

A trustor, therefore, is a person who owns property of value, and who goes through the steps necessary to create a trust of it. Stated differently, a trustor is any person who owns or has power over the use of property, who wants to dedicate it to a trust for use and consumption by one or more other persons: his beneficiaries. Without property of value, there can be no real trust. Preferably, the property should also be capable of generating useful income.

This brings us to the point of listing the essential qualifications of every serious trustor. There are five such qualifications, namely:

1. He must own one or more items of property in his own right . . . subject to any mortgages, debts, and liens thereon.
2. He must desire to create a trust, and he must want to do so willingly, thoughtfully, and knowingly; doing so because trusts are in vogue is the wrong reason.

3. He must declare his willingness in writing, and he must designate the specific property intended for the trust.

4. He must follow the trust law for uses of property in that political jurisdiction where the property or its custodian resides.

5. He must appoint a competent trustee, and one or more successor trustees, of his choosing. He is well advised to avoid appointing co-trustees (two or more persons with equal managerial authority).

So important are these five qualifications of a trustor that we summarize them in Figure 2.2. Once an item of property is in trust irrevocably, the trust becomes a valid, viable, and operating entity of its own. It is not necessary, however, that all items of property of the trustor be dedicated to a trust at the same time. He can assign some in trust during life, and other items can be assigned after death . . . by testamentary dispositions.

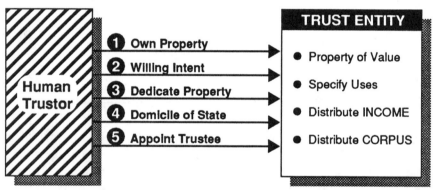

Fig. 2.2 - General Qualifications of a Trustor

Limitations on Trust Property

As you can see in Figure 2.2, the core feature of a trust is the property that is dedicated to it. Primarily, it should be income producing and capable of partitioning into "small slices" for distribution of corpus (or capital) as needed. Here, we use the term "property" in its broadest and most generalized sense. The reason we do so is that there is no statutory limitation on the specific type of property that can be transferred into trust. As long as the property is not illegally obtained by the trustor, and its intended use is not violative of public policy, there are no statutory prohibitions against the type of property assigned to a trust.

But there are certain practical limitations. Somewhere in the creative process of a trust, the "law of common sense" kicks in. Let us explain.

A trust is NOT a catchall for throwing in all kinds of odds and ends of property which the trustor may have accumulated throughout his life. That is, a trust is not a dumping site for worthless items that should have been trashed or discarded long ago. Nor is it a receptacle for everything in a trustor's estate which has some value, but which has been collected haphazardly and without culling over the years.

From an operating point of view, it is better to have only a few items of trust property, where each has significant value, than to have many multiple items of small value. This is because there are a lot of bookkeeping, accounting, and tax chores with trust property. To save costs and minimize errors, it is better to manage three to five major items of property than 30 to 50 items comprising the same total value.

For example, suppose you own 25 different stock issues in Corporate America. Before transferring (and titling) each issue into your trust, wouldn't it be better to sell them all (pay the tax), or exchange them (and pay no tax), and reacquire shareholding interests in a single mutual fund or a single brokerage firm (comprising essentially the same stocks)? Thoughtful and prudent trustors do these things well in advance of their trust creation.

A trustor obviously cannot dedicate property which he does not own in his own right. This creates problems when there is co-ownership of the same property intended for different trusts. Not all co-owners may wish to participate in a trust venture. In this situation, a trustor has to either convince the other co-owner or co-owners to participate, or else have his share of the property partitioned into his own separate name.

Once a property item belongs to a sole trustor, his only legal requirement is that it be properly titled in the official name of the trust. The legality of the titling is more forthright if the intended property is free of mortgages, liens, or other indebtedness.

Preferred Types of Property

Fundamentally, trust property is to be conserved and distributed to beneficiaries. A "beneficiary" MUST be a human person. It cannot be an entity, animal, or plant. (There are exceptions for charitable donees.) Some person must receive the income and capital from the trust for his/her maintenance, support, and pleasure. Although beneficiaries have no say in the selection and management of trust property, they invariably want their distributive share in the form of *pure money*. This beneficiary preference pretty well circumscribes the types of property most suitable for personal trusts benefiting family members down the line.

The age-old preferred-type property in a trust is real estate: land and its improvements. Land can continue forever and can be passed on from generation to generation. Indeed this is the very origin of the trust concept. However, raw, undeveloped land in and of itself is not as preferred as developed or developable land. Developed or developable land is that which is capable of producing money (income and capital) for the beneficiaries. Raw, pristine, idle land does not do this.

Developed/developable land produces money in two ways. One is through *rents*; the other is through *royalties*. Rents are periodic payments for the use of land for residential, commercial, farming, or recreational purposes. Royalties are percentage payments for the extraction of natural resources from the land (oil, gas, geothermal, coal, minerals, gravel, etc.). Most land, unfortunately, tends to be an illiquid asset when there arises a dire need for immediate money.

A second preferred type of property in trust is that which produces income through interest, dividends, and capital gains. This is the domain of stocks, bonds, Treasury notes, trust deeds, mutual fund shares, and other forms of intangible — though liquid — assets. These items are broadly classed as *marketable securities*.

A third type of preferred property is an active business which can continue as such under the auspices of the trustee. Insolvent, dormant, or bankrupt businesses obviously are not desired. But any moderately successful business — be it in proprietorship, partnership, or corporate form — qualifies. The type of business, such as manufacturing, sales, service, farming, mining, etc. is not as important as its "going concern" value. This implies the ability to appreciate in value over time.

A fourth and last priority type of property in trust involves antiques, art, and collectibles. Since these items generate no regular income on their own, their value to a trust lies strictly in their high appreciation potential This potential arises from their rarity, long history, and nonreproducibility. When these items do appreciate in value, the expectation is that they will be sold strategically. The money generated is then either distributed to the beneficiaries or "reinvested" in real estate, marketable securities, and/or active businesses.

If you, as a trustor, plan on transferring anything else than the above into trust property, you have missed the point and purpose of a trust. You have to think of a trust as a money-producing machine, much in the same way that any business is run. The management of trust property, after all, is a separate form of business of its own.

Trustee Qualifications

For trust estates over $1,000,000 (1 million), a trustor has an obligation — to himself as well as to his beneficiaries — to select a trustee for more than figurehead purposes. He has a right to expect that his trust will go on for a period of years, and that it will be administered soundly, efficiently, and with minimal recourse to trust professionals. Surely, within his extended family and relatives he can find someone who is capable and willing. Among these persons, he should select one or more with purpose and care.

We present in Figure 2.3 an outline of the criteria we believe are essential when selecting a trustee. For one thing, the person or persons should be at least over the age of 35. This is to assure some maturity when making business-type decisions with other people's money. Most preferably, a selectee should not be a beneficiary. A person who is both a trustee and a beneficiary has a natural conflict of interest. On this basis alone, a trustee-beneficiary can be a source of consternation to other "equal rights" beneficiaries. Each person selected as a trustee should have some background and experience in business, accounting, and financial affairs. Certainly, a selectee should be able to balance a checkbook without overdrawing it.

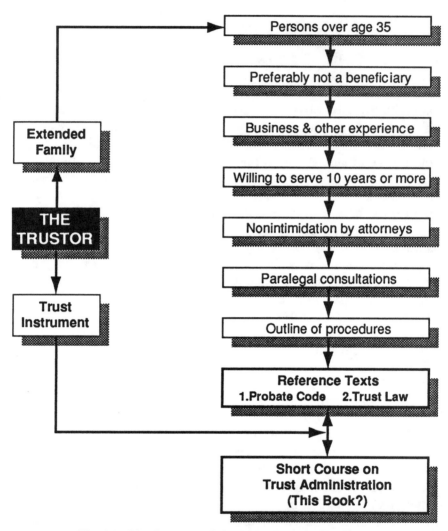

Fig. 2.3 - The Selection Criteria for Serious Trustees

Another qualification, we believe, is that a trustee has had some paralegal experience of his own. By this we mean someone who has filed papers in small claims court, traffic court, bankruptcy court, city/county offices, and attended tax audits. Even someone who has visited the probate court just to sit in on some other executor/trustee's case, and who has read the court notices on the public bulletin boards, is a good trustee candidate.

With one or more candidate trustees in mind, the next step for a trustor is to test each candidate's initiative and ability to take charge. He can do this by suggesting that each candidate preconsult with one or more paralegal services. In most metropolitan areas today, paralegals abound. Look in the phone directory. Have each candidate trustee check out his own choice of a paralegal consultant. Then the trustor should request that each of his candidates prepare an outline of the preliminary steps necessary for validating the trust upon his demise.

On trust preconsultation matters, attorneys are not very helpful. They are trained to pick at flaws in everything. Often, they will taunt and stalk trustee candidates to intimidate them out of their appointed roles. Thus, *nonintimidation by attorneys* is another important selection criterion for trustees.

Only as a last resort should one consider a trust professional as his choice for a trustee. Trust professionals — attorneys and bank trust departments particularly — tend to "take over." They are more beholden to the legal system than they are to the beneficiaries. Only designated beneficiaries have exclusive rights to the trust property. But don't shut out attorneys altogether. They *will be* needed at some point throughout the life of any trust.

Trust Instrument: General Contents

The glue that holds property in trust together is the trust instrument. The term "instrument" means any enforceable written agreement between two or more persons: trustor, trustee, beneficiaries, and (possibly) others. The instrument should contain matters of substance only. Ideally, it should be — but seldom is — devoid of legal puffery and boilerplate.

Certain key elements must be included in a trust instrument before it is legally enforceable. Among the more common content requirements are the following:

1. The name of the trustor and a declaration of his creative intent. This is usually set forth in a preamble statement.
2. The name and domicile of the trust entity, with specific reference to the law of which state shall apply.

3. A description of the specific property intended to be dedicated irrevocably to the trust entity.

4. A specific clarification of the trustor's ownership interest in property (and title form) where there is more than one owner of that property. This is particularly important for community property, joint tenancy property, tenants by entirety property, tenants in common property, and co-ownership of ongoing businesses.

5. A description of the contemplated use of the property for the generation of income and capital for distribution to beneficiaries.

6. The name and status of each beneficiary and successor beneficiary, and his/her relationship to the trustor.

7. The appointment of an initial trustee and successor trustees, by name and domicile of each. The practice of appointing co-trustees is discouraged where there are possible conflicts in management style and accounting discipline.

8. A description of the powers, duties, and liabilities of the trustee, with a "hold harmless" clause for management errors and losses when acting in good faith.

9. A procreational clause indicating the specific generational sequence of beneficiaries to be serviced by the trust. Except for the first generation of beneficiaries where death is the cutoff for distributions, successive generational cutoffs should be based upon attaining a specific age.

10. A clearly defined termination clause, directing when and how the trust shall be terminated. Without this clause, a trust runs the risk of being taxed as a corporation, rather than as a trust.

Of all the content requirements above, the keymost desirable features of a trust instrument are its clarity and specificity. These characteristics comprise the mechanism — the heart and lifebeat, if you will — that makes a trust work or not work. Unfortunately, most trust instruments are cluttered with endless contingencies, legal trivia, and quagmire clauses that work to thwart the best intentions of the trustor. Lack of clarity, readability, and comprehension is a shortcoming of all trusts. We have no magic solution to the problem. All we can do is offer encouragement to each trustee to develop his/her own keen insight and spirit of inquiry to spot the good and disregard the bad.

Meaning of "Power of Appointment"

One of the most dangerous and least understood features of trust activities is the term "power of appointment." The term applies to the power of any person having a financial interest in the trust to **appoint/take** unto himself any part of the trust property. The taking/appointing of property refers to the trust corpus or principal only. It does not refer to the periodic income of the trust which is used to pay legitimate expenses and debts, and proper distributions. It is the invasion of the corpus or principal that can sap the vitality and credibility of a trust.

There are four categories of persons who have a financial interest in a trust. These are: (1) trustors, (2) trustees, (3) beneficiaries, and (4) trust preparers. Lenders, borrowers, creditors, suppliers, or other persons or entities engaged in ordinary business transactions with a trust are not "financial interests" (in the beneficial sense). They have customary legal rights outside of the trust instrument for recovering their costs of goods and services rendered to any of the financial interests.

A power of appointment slips into the trust instrument sometimes inadvertently, and sometimes surreptitiously. Trust preparers — usually attorneys — try to be too clever. They seek to cover every conceivable contingency in the distant future that might require special access to the trust property. They thereby insert various contingency clauses interpretable as powers of appointment. It is not that powers of appointment are never allowed. It is just that any appointive power must be restricted, constrained, and limited to a specific purpose involving unusual circumstances.

For example, as a trust beneficiary, a surviving spouse or handicapped child of the trustor may be granted a *limited* power of appointment. Such power authorizes invasion of the trust corpus for such contingencies as—

(1)   Continuing his/her customary support.

(2)   Defraying major medical and hospital expenses.

(3)   Meeting special education and rehabilitation needs.

Where no special circumstances are prescribed for access to the trust corpus, and there are clauses that imply any power of appointment, said power is construed to be a general power.

There is grave danger in general power of appointment clauses in a trust instrument. Such power can defeat the purpose of a trust and deplete its assets prematurely. Not only this, but the person ascribed as having said power is treated as the legal owner of the trust property. He is so treated — and taxed — whether he exercises said power or not.

So dangerous is the power of appointment concept to the vitality of a trust that we feel compelled to present a depiction of it. Accordingly, we present Figure 2.4. The point that we want to get across is that, if you are a trustor or trustee, you must exercise great care to prevent any general powers of appointment from creeping into your trust documentation.

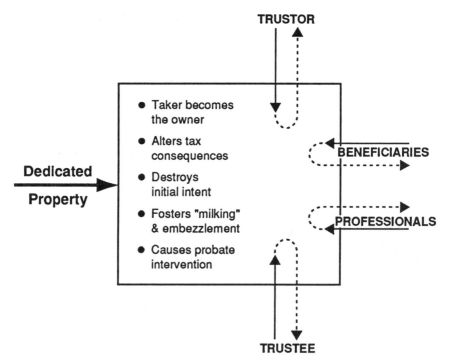

Fig. 2.4 - Power of Appointment Dangers in a Trust

How Trustees Are Weakened

One of the truly fascinating features of a trust is its facility for passing money and property on from generation to generation. Indeed, this is the intent of most trusts created by persons of power, privilege, and wealth. They regard their trust arrangement as a mechanism for creating ongoing life into eternity. Property — and the income from it — is passed on and on. In the generational process, the initial trustee is replaced by a successor trustee, who in turn is replaced by a successor trustee . . . and so on.

Ordinarily, the generational "on and on" succession is limited only by the staying value of the initial property transferred into the trust. Obviously, a $1 million estate will become exhausted long before a $100 million estate.

Fostering this ongoing generational concept is a provision in the Internal Revenue Code [namely, Section 2631] which allows a one-million-dollar exemption when skipping over any one generation to another. This allowance is called: the *GST exemption.* (The "GST" stands for: Generation Skipping Transfer.) For the purpose of this exemption, a "generation" comprises the lineal descendants of the trustor at 25-year intervals.

Tax conscious trust preparers fan these GST exemptions into very complex clauses of successive generations yet unborn. We refer to these clauses as procreational and perpetuity interests. We object to these clauses because they weaken the powers and obscure the duties of conscientious trustees. There are too many branching interests at stake. After the third or fourth generation, it is not uncommon for 25 to 50 beneficial interests to be involved.

Our real objection to procreational/perpetuity clauses in a trust is that they encourage fee milking by trust professionals. Once a trustor is deceased, and his first generation of trustees and beneficiaries passes on, the second, third, and subsequent generations are at the sole mercy of the trust professionals and the legal system where the trust property is administered. Many a trust has been prematurely depleted by legal professionals. This is because the second, third, and subsequent successor trustees become successively intimidated by the legal system. All too sadly they eventually succumb to it.

Consequently, we think that no more than three generations of beneficiaries should ever be contemplated in a trust instrument. This group comprises the children of the trustor, his grandchildren, and great grandchildren. It is even doubtful that the great grandchildren will remember the trustor and what he stood for in life. This includes the third successor trustee as well.

Check Your Trust Law

There is a positive way to avoid being intimidated by attorneys and their legal system. Review the trust law in that state where the trust instrument is validated. As mentioned earlier, trust law is usually found in your state's probate code. If you have access to a pubic library, visit and ask to be directed to its legal section. Retrieve the latest edition of the probate code and browse through it.

In the California Probate Code, for example, Trust Law is found in the section headed: *Creation, Validity, Modification, and Termination of Trusts*. A few excerpts from this volume are helpful in recognizing the key legal characteristics of a valid trust.

Selected excerpts (with emphasis added) are:

1. A trust is created only if the settlor [trustor] *properly manifests an intention to create a trust.* [¶ 15201]

2. A trust is created only if there is trust property. [¶ 15202]

3. A trust may be created for any purpose that is not illegal or against public policy. [¶ 15203]

4. A trust . . . is created only if there is a beneficiary. This requirement is satisfied if the trust instrument provides for either of the following:

(a) A beneficiary or class of beneficiaries that is ascertainable with reasonable certainty or that is sufficiently described so it can be determined that some person meets the description or is within the class.

(b)   A grant of a power to the trustee or some other person to select the beneficiaries based on a standard or in the discretion of the trustee or other person. [¶ 15205]

5. If the trust instrument provides that a beneficiary's interest in **income** is not subject to voluntary or involuntary transfer, the beneficiary's interest in income under the trust may not be transferred and is not subject to enforcement of a money judgment until paid to the beneficiary. [¶ 15300]

6. If the trust instrument provides that a beneficiary's interest in **principal** [corpus] is not subject to voluntary or involuntary transfer, the beneficiary's interest in principal may not be transferred and is not subject to enforcement of a money judgment until paid to the beneficiary. [¶ 15301]

7. Unless a trust instrument is expressly made irrevocable by the trust instrument, the trust is revocable by the settlor. This applies only where the settlor is domiciled in this state when the trust is created, where the trust instrument is executed in this state, or where the trust instrument provides that the law of this state governs the trust. [¶ 15400]

8. If all beneficiaries of an irrevocable trust consent, they may compel modification or termination of the trust upon petition to the [probate] court. [¶ 15403]

9. A trust terminates when any of the following occurs:

    (a)   The term of the trust expires.
    (b)   The trust purpose is fulfilled.
    (c)   The trust purpose becomes unlawful.
    (d)   The trust purpose becomes impossible to fulfill.
    (e)   The trust is revoked. [¶ 15407]

10. The statutory rule against perpetuities . . . seeks to disallow . . . any interest or trust beyond . . . the expiration of a period of time not exceeding 21 years after the death of the

survivor of specified lives in being at the creation of the trust or other property arrangement. [¶ 21209]

Uneconomical Trusts

The California Probate Code raises and addresses the concept of uneconomical trusts. The section is 15408, and is titled: ***Trusts With Uneconomical Low Principal.*** It is instructive to share with you in full this section.

Accordingly, Section 15408 reads as follows:

(a) On petition by a trustee or beneficiary if the court determines that the fair market value of the principal of a trust has become so low in relation to the cost of administration that continuation of the trust under its existing terms will defeat or substantially impair the accomplishment of its purposes, the court may, in its discretion and in a manner that conforms as nearly as possible to the intention of the settlor [trustor], *order any of the following—*

(1) Termination of the trust.
(2) Modification of the trust.
(3) Appointment of a new trustee.

(b) Notwithstanding subdivision (a), if the trust principal does not exceed twenty thousand dollars ($20,000) in value, the trustee has the power to terminate the trust.

This addressing of uneconomical trusts conveys judicial and practical wisdom. It recognizes that the popular practice of having a trust for prestige purposes is not welcomed. There has to be some administrative practicality in terms of the dollar value of the trust property. Although the above section designates $20,000 as a statutory minimum, we think $100,000 is a more realistic threshold. Creating a trust with a lesser amount than this doesn't make much sense. You'll understand more why we say this when we get into later chapters.

3

LEGAL DUTIES OF TRUSTEE

An Independent-Minded Trustee Should Procure On His Own A COMPACT EDITION Of The Applicable State Law Prescribing His Many Legal Duties. Among These, His Focal Duty Is To Collect, Hold, Separate, And Administer The Trust Property Prudently. Conflicts Of Interest Are To Be Avoided. Trustee Loyalty To The Beneficiaries Is Key, Followed By Reports Of Account Periodically. Altogether, There Are Some 30 Duties To The Beneficiaries And 30 Powers Over The Trust Property. For These Services, There Must Be Adequate Compensation. Breach Of Trust Can Result In Removal Of The Violative Trustee.

No matter how much money and property a trustor may have, no matter how clear and specific his trust instrument is, the success of a trust rests squarely and exclusively upon the trustee. If the trustee is alert to the conservational and distributive needs of the beneficiaries, and he properly accounts to them for his actions, he will have served his trustor well. A trustee must be loyal to his trustor while, at the same time, he is duty bound to the beneficiaries. The result is that every trustee is placed "in the middle" of all trust operations, once the trust property becomes irrevocable therein.

All trustees have a duty to perform well and account to the beneficiaries. A trustee must NOT engage in trust transactions for his/her own account. Poor management control and conflicts of interest invariably lead to breach of trust. When this occurs, legal action can be taken against the trustee.

Where there is a breach of trust, the responsible trustee can be compelled to make restitution. He can be directed (by the probate court) to restore depleted value to the property; he can be deprived of compensation; or he can be removed as trustee. In all proper respects, a trustee is fully liable for his negligence and mismanagement of trust affairs. He has discretionary powers . . . but he has liabilities, too. These are matters which we classify as the *legal duties* of a trustee. They are separate and apart, yet intertwined with, his management, accounting, and tax duties.

Especially for trust estates over $1 million, the duties, powers, and liabilities of a trustee become serious matters indeed. This is because there are legal responsibilities imposed on a trustee by state law. In this chapter, therefore, we want to review the legal aspects of trustee duties by using excerpts from the California Probate Code: Trust Law division. Whether you are — or may be — a trustor, trustee, or beneficiary, your financial interests in the trust property depend on the faithful attention to detail by the trustee. Included in this attention is the trustee having a watchful eye out for disgruntled beneficiaries and "attorneys in the woodwork."

Beware of Covetous Attorneys

When managing trust property worth millions of dollars, there are a lot of hawks "out there" who want to tap into it somehow, and start milking it. Being a trustee for such amounts is a natural target of professional envy. There is one particular profession where this envy can rise to the point of avaricious attacks on the modus operandi of the trustee. This is the legal profession: attorneys et al.

All matters of wills, trusts, estates, and property conveyances are regarded by the legal profession as its sole and exclusive domain. While attorneys recognize — most reluctantly — that every trustor has the inherent right to appoint a trustee of his choosing (who is a nonattorney), they seethe . . . and stew . . . and scheme. They look for the minuteness of flaw to jump in and take over. If they can't find such a flaw, they manufacture one by raising cobweb questions and thoughts in the mind of some less informed beneficiary. Since each beneficiary is a part-owner (beneficially) of the trust property, covetous attorneys can get at the trustee through such persons.

Ask yourself this question. Why would an attorney (not every attorney, of course) scheme so to attack, discredit, and displace an appointed trustee?

The answer is simple: MONEY — sometimes big money. Aggressive attorneys view a trust estate as their *entitlement program* for commission milking and fee milking for as long as the trust exists. They think in terms of statutory commissions (about 2% annually) and extraordinary fees (about $350 per hour). You should think of this as legalized "grave robbing." After all, when a trustor is deceased, it is the legal profession and state law which has the final say. The "final say" can be stretched out until the trust estate is dissipated.

Obviously, it is in the best interests of the legal profession that figurehead trustees be appointed, rather than trustees who are independent-minded. Figurehead trustees will call on attorneys at the drop of a pin; independent trustees will not. Nevertheless, independent trustees are — or should be — prudent enough to call on attorneys when a bona fide situation truly requires special expertise.

Please do not misread the above. What we are trying to say is that, because of the many legal duties imposed by state law on trustees, there is likely to be some attorney out there keeping an eye on you. He is eyeing your job . . . and the trust property. To some extent, this is ordinary human nature. But the egregiousness of this behavior is more pronounced in the legal profession than in any other. We just want you to be aware of this, that's all. Keep your own watchful eye on the woodwork.

Compact Edition of Trust Law

Whenever a breach-of-duty issue is alleged involving a trustee, the matter is pursued in probate court in the state having jurisdiction over the trust instrument or trust property. Every trust instrument has a clause somewhere in it to this effect. This makes practical sense. Whenever legitimate disputes arise concerning a trust and its trustee, there has to be some mutually respected arbitration source.

This is one of the ancillary roles of probate proceedings. Consequently, every independent trustee should have at least some familiarity with such proceedings.

The best way to obtain this familiarity (*without* an attorney) is to procure on your own behalf a "compact edition" of the probate and trust law for the state of jurisdiction. Various legal publishing firms prepare such editions. To find out, go on line or phone or visit your county law library or county bar association. Said editions usually are soft cover and cost about $35 per copy. They cite every pertinent probate and trust law, with cross-references to other laws, such as: Construction (and interpretation) of Wills, Trusts, and Other Instruments.

For example, in the compact edition of the California Probate Code (CPC), Part 5 of its trust law is titled: *Judicial Proceedings Concerning Trusts*. It covers such matters as jurisdiction and venue, serving of notices, filing of petitions, grounds for hearings, appeal from rulings, transfer of jurisdiction, etc. As an instructive excerpt, CPC ¶ 17006 on jury trials says—

> There is **no right to a jury trial** in proceedings under this division [Division 9: Trust Law] concerning the internal affairs of trusts. [Emphasis added.]

This "no right to a jury trial" implies that an independent trustee can petition or respond on his own, without being represented by an attorney. Proceedings in this case are somewhat less formal than otherwise would be expected of jury trials.

Having a compact edition of trust law at each trustee's fingertips is a tremendous confidence builder. It provides a handy source for checking on popular statements and misstatements concerning the operation of trusts. It also tempers the extent of intimidation that some attorneys try to use to pressure and taunt a trustee into giving up. In addition to browsing through and becoming familiar with trust law organization, every trustee MUST read — and reread, as necessary — the particular part titled: *Trust Administration*. It is here that one will find the legally prescribed duties, powers, and liabilities of all trustees.

Digest of Prescribed Duties

Using California as an example, we list in Figure 3.1 selected trustee duties that are prescribed by Sections 16000 through 16082 of that state's trust law. We urge that you take a moment and scan down the listing. The referenced "CPC ¶" designations are California Probate Code Section Numbers.

CPC¶	DUTY	DESCRIPTION
16000	Administer Trust	According to trust instrument
16002	Be Loyal	Solely to interests of beneficiaries
16003	Be Impartial	When two or more beneficiaries
16004	Avoid Conflicts	No "self-dealing" with trust property
16006	Control & Preserve	Dispose of unproductive property
16009	Identify Assets	Distinct separation of trust property
16010	Enforce Claims	Of trust property against others
16011	Defend Actions	Of others against trust property
16012	Do Not Delegate	Do acts oneself or supervise others
16040	Prudent Care	At all times re trust purposes
16041	Compensation	Not to affect performance
16060	Must Inform	Keep in touch with beneficiaries
16062	Accounting	Provide periodically full reports
16063	Report Contents	Receipts, disbursements, assets, etc.
16080	Discretionary Power	Shall be "exercised reasonably"

Fig. 3.1 - Digest of Trustee Duties in California

As you see in Figure 3.1, there are 15 different duties listed. Altogether there are 30 different official duties prescribed. Some are self-explanatory, some are not. Others require special focus so that you will not overlook the scope of attention needed. Can you imagine a figurehead trustee being familiar with all the duties officially prescribed? Would not an independent-minded trustee be more likely to dig in and take hold?

The very first listing in Figure 3.1 is the duty to administer the trust. This duty, prescribed by CPC ¶ 16000, reads in full as—

On acceptance of the trust, the trustee has a duty to administer the trust according to the trust instrument and, except to the extent the trust instrument provides otherwise, according to this division [of trust law].

If you examine this duty closely, you will see that three preconditions are involved. Foremost is that the trust instrument (agreement) must be accepted by the trustee, before his duty becomes enforceable. This means that a trustee, even though selected by the trustor and named as such in the trust instrument, has the right to back out of the deal before he initially takes charge. If he does decide to back out, he must notify the successor trustee.

Once a trustee accepts responsibility for administering a trust, he must follow the instructions in the trust instrument. This is the second precondition for assuming a trustee's duty. This means that, with respect to the trust property and its distributions, he does **not** have to follow instructions from the beneficiaries. He must, of course, be mindful of their wishes and be as diplomatic as possible with them. But he is not duty bound to the beneficiaries where their demands counter the provisions in the trust instrument.

There is a third precondition for accepting one's duty as a trustee. The trust instrument may require the performance of other duties, over and above those prescribed in the trust law of the state of jurisdiction. So long as these additional duties (to those in Figure 3.1) do not contradict or negate the statutorily assigned duties, they are enforceable. Obviously, the trust instrument cannot require a trustee to perform an illegal act.

On the matter of trust property, it should be self-evident that—

The trustee has a duty:

(a) To keep the trust property separate from other property not subject to the trust.

(b) To see that the trust property is designated as property of the trust. [CPC ¶ 16009.]

Where trust property is commingled with marital property, co-owned property, encumbered property, and other ownership and titling uncertainties, the duty to separate and designate the trust property can be a Herculean task. A thoughtful trustor would try to clarify these matters before his demise.

Avoid Conflicts of Interest

Because a trustee is the sole custodian and manager of trust property, he has one paramount duty above all others. He must avoid and restrain himself against conflicts of interest. A "conflict" is any self-dealing — or perceived self-dealing — between the trustee and the trust property. When one controls property worth millions of dollars, it is awfully tempting at times to "borrow" from that property to defray the personal obligations and lifestyle of the trustee. Extreme self-discipline is required to resist these temptations. This is why only *financially mature* trustees should be chosen by the trustor.

Once a trustor is deceased, the trust property belongs exclusively to the beneficiaries. A trustee's duty therewith is to administer said property—

. . . solely in the interest of the beneficiaries. [CPC ¶ 16002.]

A trustee should never forget this.

To make sure that he doesn't, specific transactional prohibitions are prescribed in law. Pursuant to CPC ¶ 16004 and ¶ 16005, portions of these prohibitions read [emphasis supplied]:

*(1) The trustee has a duty **not to use or deal with** trust property for the trustee's own profit or for any other purpose unconnected with the trust, nor to take part in any transaction in which the trustee has an interest adverse to the beneficiary.*

*(2) A transaction between the **trustee and a beneficiary** which occurs during the existence of the trust or while the trustee's influence with the beneficiary remains and by which the trustee*

obtains an advantage from the beneficiary is presumed to be a violation of the trustee's fiduciary responsibilities.

*(3) The trustee of one trust has a duty not to knowingly become a trustee of another trust **adverse in its nature** to the interest of the beneficiary of the first trust, and a duty to eliminate the conflict or resign as trustee when the conflict is discovered.*

In other words, a trustee has the duty to police himself . . . or to resign. This means that, at all transactional times, he must be sensitive to those activities which adversely affect beneficiary interests. The fundamental premise here is 100% loyalty to the beneficiaries. Such loyalty, therefore, is **the** sacred ingredient of every successful trust.

The "Prudent Person" Standard

Though it is well and good to insist on absolute loyalty to the beneficiaries, the trustee still has a duty to administer the property. Unless the property is never to be altered from its initial trust form, the trustee must engage in business-type transactions. This means that he has to engage in offering, selling, exchanging, acquiring, investing, borrowing, expensing, modifying, restoring, and other active business efforts. In so doing, ordinary business risks are always at stake. Consequently, the duty of loyalty does not mean a guarantee against downside risks in property transactions. Not all beneficiaries understand ordinary business risks.

To protect the trustee against beneficiary-perceived acts of disloyalty, the California trust code prescribes a Standard of Care Rule. The rationale is that there is a reasonable standard of performance expected by persons who are not influenced by their own self-interests. This rationale is called the "prudent person" rule.

In CPC ¶ 16040, the standard-of-care rule reads in pertinent part as follows:

*(a) The trustee shall administer the trust with care, skill, prudence, and diligence **under the circumstances then***

prevailing that a prudent person acting in a like capacity and familiar with such matters would use in the conduct of an enterprise of like character and with like aims to accomplish the purposes of the trust as determined from the trust instrument.

(b) When investing, reinvesting, purchasing, acquiring, exchanging, selling, and managing trust property, the trustee shall act with care, skill, prudence, and diligence under the circumstances then prevailing, including but not limited to the general economic conditions and the anticipated needs of the trust and its beneficiaries. . . . [Emphasis added.]

In the real world, after a transaction has turned out to be unprofitable, hindsight brings out the worst in people. This is particularly true with attorneys, and also true with misguided beneficiaries.

In defense, the trustee must show that he acted in good faith at all times. This incudes a showing of the use of intelligent judgment, based on the actual facts and circumstances. A showing of good faith and due diligence exonerates the trustee from blame for his transactional losses and below-average results.

Reports of Account

It is the duty of a trustee to keep the beneficiaries reasonably informed on the status of the trust property. This should be done at least annually, and on other occasions when so requested by the beneficiaries. The vehicle for doing so is a "report of account" on the assets, liabilities, receipts, and disbursements of the trust.

As pursuant to CPC ¶ 16063, the contents of each accounting shall consist of the following (with emphasis added):

(a) A statement of receipts and disbursements of principal and income that have occurred during the last complete fiscal year of the trust or since the last account.

(b) A statement of the assets and liabilities of the trust as of . . . the end of the period covered by the account.

*(c)   The **trustee's compensation** [and expenses] . . . since the last account.*

*(d)   The **agents hired** by the trustee, their relationship to the trustee, if any, and their compensation.*

*(e)   A statement that the recipient of the account may **petition the court** . . . to obtain a court review of the account and of the acts of the trustee.*

*(f)   A statement that **claims against the trustee** for breach of trust may not be made after the expiration of **three years** from the date the beneficiary receives an account or report disclosing facts giving rise to the claim.*

A prudent trustee tries to go along with the wishes of the beneficiaries as much as he can. But he is not beholden to them with regard to their every suggestion for investments, accounting procedures, and the use of agents by the trust. In fact, one of his duties is not to delegate to anyone that which he can reasonably do on his own. [CPC ¶ 16012.]

When presenting the annual report of accounts, it is recommended that the trustee meet with all of the beneficiaries collectively. This gives him an opportunity to explain what he did during the year and get their feedback. Straight talk and two-way communications are particularly important where transactional results with the trust property have been less than exciting. This is also opportunity for the trustee to get a "feel" as to which of the beneficiaries, if any, perceives him as being in breach of trust. It is imprudent to wait three years to find out what some stalking beneficiary really thinks.

Many Trustee Powers

To carry out their duties, trustees are granted many powers of discretion and judgment in the management of trust property. There are two categories of these powers: general powers and specific powers. The general powers address the source of authority for

LEGAL DUTIES OF TRUSTEE

power, whereas the specific powers address the day-to-day business operations of the trust.

In California, for example, the basic trust law on general powers is Section 16200 [CPC]. This law, in full, reads—

A trustee has the following powers without the need to obtain court authorization:

(a)   The powers conferred by the trust instrument.
(b)   Except as limited in the trust instrument, the powers conferred by statute.
(c)   Except as limited in the trust instrument, the power to perform any act that a trustee would perform for the purposes of the trust under the standard of care provided in Section 16040 [previously cited].

As is evident above, the core of the trustee's power train is the trust instrument itself. This is why this instrument should be created with great skill and expertise. This is where the role of trust professionals in preparing the trust instrument proves their worth.

When a trust instrument imposes a condition which interferes with or restricts a trustee's exercise of general power, he can petition the (probate) court for relief from such restriction. He can also petition the court for interpretive guidance on matters in the trust instrument which are unclear, ambiguous, or unrealistic. Thus, in one sense, a trustee has power in his own right to question the duties and conditions imposed on him by the trust instrument. Under the veil of his fiduciary duties, a trustee cannot be expected to accomplish that which is impossible.

Specific Statutory Powers

As to a trustee's specific powers to manage the trust property, there are many, many of them. Altogether, there are at least some 30 of these powers. We list these in edited form in Figure 3.2. They are taken directly from California trust law, Sections 16220 through 16249. We've tried to make the listing as self-explanatory

CPC¶	POWER	CPC¶	POWER
16220	Collect & hold property	16235	Calls & assessments
16221	Accept additions	16236	Stock conversions
16222	Continue existing business	16237	Change business form
16223	Make investments	16238	Hold securities
16224	U.S. Gov. Bonds	16239	Deposit securities
16225	Insure deposits	16240	Carry insurance
16226	Buy/sell property	16241	Borrow money
16227	Manage & control	16242	Pay claims
16228	Encumber property	16243	Pay expenses
16229	Make alterations	16244	Lend money
16230	Develop land	16245	Make distributions
16231	Incur leases	16246	Adjust distributions
16232	Mineral rights	16247	Hire persons
16233	Grant options	16248	Execute documents
16234	Voting rights	16249	Prosecute wrong

Fig. 3.2 - The "30 Powers" of Trustees in California

as possible. We have no intention of stepping you through each of the 30 powers separately.

As you can infer from the Figure 3.2 listing, they represent exactly what an owner of any property item could do with his own property. A properly empowered trustee can do the same. The only omissions from Figure 3.2 are personal enjoyment of the trust property by the trustee, deriving pecuniary benefit for himself, and gifting/bequeathing any of the property to his own heirs. Otherwise, statutorily, the trustee can undertake any business transaction that he needs to, to carry out the purposes of a trust.

The core substance and rationale of a trustee's specific powers is expressed in CPC ¶ 16226: *Acquisition and Disposition of Property*. This one-sentence trust law reads exactly as—

The trustee has the power to acquire or dispose of property, for cash or on credit, at public or private sale, or by exchange.

Anyone who has the legal power to buy and sell property certainly has all the authority he needs to administer a trust estate. This includes borrowing money, obtaining insurance, changing form of business, making loans to beneficiaries, development of land, executing legal papers . . . on and on. These are the types of statutory provisions found in the trust law of every state where trust property is under its jurisdiction.

Back in Chapter 1 we questioned why most trust instruments are loaded with boiler-plate recitation of the duties and powers of trustees. Such procedure makes for a more lengthy trust document without really adding to that which already exists in trust law. Consequently, our contention is that these recitations, in standardized form, could be an Appendix A: Duties and Powers of Trustees, attached to every trust instrument. The applicable trust law sections could be shown for cross-referencing. This way, a trust preparer could concentrate more on the trustor's distributive instructions rather than on voluminous legalese.

Not many persons question the statutory duties and powers of trustees. This is because there is universal acceptance that such powers are needed. However, the trust instrument may provide for still other powers. The most common of these relate to the frequency and magnitude of the income and capital distributions to the beneficiaries. The state of mind of the trustor may have been that he wants his trustee to spoon-feed or incentive-feed a beneficiary or two, for each beneficiary's own good. The most important practical power is that a trustee be authorized to do this when conditions warrant. A spendthrift beneficiary can be quite demanding and totally obnoxious.

Compensation for Services

From the foregoing, it should be evident that the larger the estate, the more asset-diverse it is, and the more beneficiaries involved, the more services are required by the trustee. He is to be compensated for his services and for his loyalty. Even if a trustee is a blood-relative of the trustor or beneficiaries, he should not be expected to serve free. We depict this compensation justification in Figure 3.3.

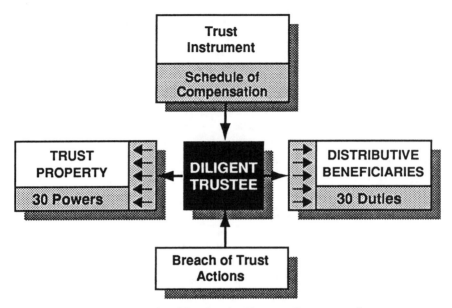

Fig. 3.3 - The Justification for Trustee Compensation

A farsighted trustor should be aware of the need for compensating his trustee(s). As such, he has a duty to provide in the trust instrument some plan or schedule of compensation. The schedule may consist of one or more of the following compensation forms:

1. a periodic base fee,
2. a percentage of the trust net worth,
3. a minimum flat fee,
4. a specific hourly rate,
5. a per transaction charge, or
6. special fee for extraordinary services.

Where a trust instrument does not specify any compensation, a trustee has three options available One, he can assign himself a reasonable fee and disclose the amount on his reports of account to the beneficiaries. This is clearly so implied in California trust law, Section 15681, to wit:

If the trust instrument does not specify the trustee's compensation, the trustee is entitled to reasonable compensation under the circumstances.

A second option is for the trustee to propose to the beneficiaries a fee schedule which he believes is commensurate with the tasks performed. When doing this, it is helpful to obtain and present the fee schedules in other trusts of a similar nature.

A third option is for the trustee to petition the probate court to establish a fee arrangement for his services. In this regard, CPC ¶ 15680 and ¶ 15682 state quite clearly that—

Upon proper showing, the court may fix or allow greater or lesser compensation than could be allowed under the terms of the trust. . . . The court may [also] fix an amount of periodic compensation . . . to continue for as long as the court determines is proper.

Thus, a trustee's right to compensation is a fundamental part of trust law. In addition, a trustee has the right to expect repayment for any expenditures that he incurs out of his own pocket for the benefit of the trust. The repayment for expenses, as well as the payment of compensation for services, are made from the trust property. As a matter of law, the trustee has an automatic "mechanic's lien" against the trust property for his compensation and expenses.

Breach of Trust Actions

There is no universal definition of what constitutes a breach of trust, with respect to trust property. As much as anything, it is the state of mind of the person who perceives that there has been a breach. Sometimes a recalcitrant beneficiary is egged on by cavalier friends and covetous attorneys. Certainly, a trustee's disregard of his duties, abuse of his powers, embezzlement of funds, or gross negligence would be sufficient cause for action against him.

The nearest statutory definition on point is CPC ¶ 16400 which reads in its entirety as—

> *A violation by the trustee of any duty that the trustee owes the beneficiary is a breach of trust.* [Emphasis added.]

As the emphasized phrases indicate, there are two prerequisites to a breach. One, there must be a violation of duty — *any* duty.

The second prerequisite is that a beneficiary — *the* beneficiary — be violated. The statutory use of the phrase "the beneficiary" implies a *current* beneficiary who either is receiving or who was supposed to have received benefits from the trust. Successor beneficiaries and contingent beneficiaries are not damaged until such time as they acquire the legal right to the trust property.

When a bona fide breach of trust occurs, the affected beneficiary may commence legal proceedings against the trustee. Under California law (CPC ¶ 16420), the types of remedial action that can be sought are as follows (slightly rearranged):

(1)   To compel the trustee to perform the trustee's duties.
(2)   To enjoin the trustee from committing a breach of trust.
(3)   To compel the trustee to redress a breach of trust by payment of money or otherwise.
(4)   To set aside acts of the trustee.
(5)   To impose an equitable lien on trust property.
(6)   To trace trust property that has been wrongfully disposed of and recover the property or its proceeds.
(7)   To appoint a receiver or temporary trustee to take possession of the trust property and administer the trust.
(8)   To reduce or deny compensation of the trustee.
(9)   To remove the trustee.

When a trustor-appointed trustee is judicially removed for breach of trust, it is incumbent upon the plaintiff to recommend a qualified replacement. If no replacement is suggested, the court will appoint a trustee of its own choosing. Often, the replacement is the attorney who prodded and represented the plaintiff in the breach action.

4

DISSECTING THE CONTRACT

All Trust Instruments Tend To Be Lengthy: 25-50 Pages Or So. This Is Because Of Trying To Cover All Contingencies During Life, Upon Death, And For Extended Periods Thereafter. Your Job Is To SIFT THROUGH, Deleting Those Paragraphs Which Are Inapplicable, Highlighting Those Which Are Applicable, And Extracting Those Which Are Repetitive. Focus Primarily On AFTER-DEATH-TAX Assets Which Are Directed Into The "Residuary Trust." Use Your Discretionary Powers To Minimize Complexity Caused By Multiple Trusts. Prepare Table Of Contents And "Enshrine" Your Powers . . . For Handy Reference.

For our purposes, "the contract" comprises the whole "bundle of papers" that was used for formulating the trust instrument, including, of course, the trust instrument itself. As such, it is your duty to review these things in a general way, so as to extract the essence of what your trustor had in mind. Often, the trust instrument tends to reflect more what the trust preparer had in mind, based on his interpretation of what the trustor wanted. As trustee, you have an obligation to apply *your interpretation* of what the trustor intended for the best interests of his beneficiaries. Once the trustor is deceased, you have legal authority which the trust preparer does not have.

As a trust administrator, you have to orient your thinking over a long time period: from several to many years. In this chapter, therefore, we want to focus on techniques to use to *overview* the trust instrument before you really get down to the business of administering it. Unfortunately, most trust instruments are so wordy and obfuscating that it is easy to get lost without some beacon lights along the way. Our objective is to help you dissect the contract selectively, so that you can reconstruct it in your own words. By so doing, you'll be able to schedule your work activities in a more purposeful manner, without false starts and disputive quagmires.

Photocopy the Original

As a full-fledged trustee (meaning the trust is irrevocable), you are the official custodian of the latest original trust instrument that is applicable. No one else needs this document. Check to see if it is complete in all respects. Here, the term "complete" means—

1. The trust document itself (main body)
2. All exhibits thereto (property assignments)
3. Any amendments thereto (changing specific paragraphs)

The original trust instrument should be *unmarked* in any way, with all authenticating signatures affixed, including that of a Notary Public. It should be kept by you in a separate filing arrangement of its own, readily accessible by you.

For your own dissection and examination purposes, make at least one complete copy of the original. You want to be able to mark it up, cut it up, enter reference notations, and highlight particular words and phrases that will facilitate your authority and administrative role.

In a legal document of 25 to 50 pages in length, there will be some paragraphs and pages that you may want to reproduce several times. As a "for example," one paragraph that you should want to reproduce several times would be that which is titled: *Trustee's Discretion*. The typical wording that we've excerpted from an actual (original) trust document reads—

Where, under this Agreement, the Trustee is granted discretion, the Trustee's discretion shall be sole and absolute. Any action taken or refrained from by the Trustee in good faith shall be binding upon all persons and corporations interested therein.

Make sure that any such selected paragraph is annotated with its official article, paragraph, and page number, to wit: *Article XII, Para. 12.05, p. 33.*

Having a selected paragraph like this one reproduced several times can come in handy. Sooner or later, as you become engrossed in your duties, some attorney, some accountant, some clerk, some supplier, some broker, some beneficiary, or some blood relative of the trustor will question your discretionary authority. Anticipate such questions . . . and prepare for them. One way of doing so is to have your selected paragraph reproduced on several 3"x 5" cards. When someone in the woodwork tries to insinuate improper action on your part, pull out a card and hand it to him. Do this nonchalantly. Should push come to shove, and you wind up before a probate judge, you'll be able to recite your discretionary authority from memory. You might even hand the judge a 3"x 5" card for his/her own reading.

Prepare Table of Contents

There is one glaring omission from most trust instruments, whether revocable or irrevocable. It is the lack of a cover page with table of contents. Our contention is that any trust instrument over five pages should have a Table of Contents. This is rarely done. This omission is one reason why many trustees become disoriented and confused. They read and reread paragraphs which have little substance, often missing the ones that do.

A table of contents is missing because most trust instruments are not well organized. They are generally a hodgepodge of paragraphs, sections, and articles. They are arranged in no particular logical order. Sometimes the word groupings are numbered (or lettered); sometimes they are not. Whatever the sequence, it is rare that the groups of words and phrases are accompanied by any quick-identity headings. Subject headings such as: Designation of Beneficiaries; Distribution Instructions; Compensation of Trustee; Termination of Trust; etc. are not only informative, but are an aid in spotting at a glance the subject matter of interest. Otherwise, one is forced to scan-read through every page of the trust instrument to locate a particular item of current interest.

More often than is admitted, professional trust preparers — mostly attorneys — intentionally omit identifying headings. They do this on the premise that, when a trustee does not understand the trust contents, he'll keep coming back for consultation . . . and reconsultations.

If your trust instrument has no cover page of contents — we already know it doesn't — you *must* prepare one on your own. If a paragraph, article, or section has no preparer-assigned heading, you assign one. If you do this in a diligent way, you'll be amazed what you'll learn about your own trust. By picking through the legalese in search of succinct subject matter, you may discover that your trust does not say or do what *you* thought it should say or do. So don't be at all surprised. We have forewarned you.

As an example of what we mean by preparing your own cover-page Table of Contents, we present Figure 4.1. The particular arrangement and selection of headings that we show is a composite of numerous trust instruments that we have reviewed. We have arranged the subject items to provide a more logical flow of thought than is found in most trust instruments. The hodgepodgey legalese sequence in a trust instrument is a sure sign that you will not understand what your trust is all about.

Clarify Name of Trust

It is the darnedest thing. You can skim through paragraphs and pages of a trust instrument, but you can't find the intended name of his trust when a trustor dies. Matters get even more murky when there are two spousal trustors, each authenticating a joint living trust document.

Here's an example of what we mean. The following paragraph is excerpted from an active living trust document where the husband predeceased the wife. Its Article IV is titled: *Division of Trust After Death of a Trustor*. Its paragraph 4.01 is subtitled: *Division into Three Trusts*. The first subparagraph reads verbatim:

Article	Subject	Page
	Table of Contents Coversheet	
	THE JOHN J. JONES TRUST, Dated: July 17, 2004	
I	Declaration of Trustor's Intent	1
II	Name & Jurisdiction of Trust	2
III	Initial Trust Property	3
IV	Additions to Trust Property	4
V	Appointment of Trustee	5
VI	Choice of Successor Trustee	6
VII	Designation of Beneficiaries	7
VIII	Conditions for Successor Beneficiaries	8
IX	Beneficial Purpose of Trust	10
X	Distribution of Trust Income	12
XI	Distribution of Trust Corpus	15
XII	Contingency/Discretionary Distributions	18
XIII	Powers of Trustee	20
XIV	Content of Trustee Reports	23
XV	Administrative Provisions	25
XVI	Compensation of Trustee	27
XVII	Breach of Duty of Trustee	29
XVIII	Issues for Judicial Recourse	31
XIX	Termination of Trust	33
XX	Signaturization by Trustor	35
	LIST OF EXHIBITS	

"A": Initial Trust Property, dated: _____

"B": Additional Trust Property I, dated: _____

"C": Additional Trust Property II, dated: _____

Fig. 4.1 - Example "Table of Contents" for a Trust

The first Trustor to die shall be called the "Deceased Spouse" or "Deceased Trustor" and the living Trustor shall be called the "Surviving Spouse" or "Surviving Trustor." On the death of the Deceased Trustor, the Trustee shall divide the Trust Estate, including any additions made to the Trust by his or her death, such as from the decedent's Will or by life insurance policies on the decedent's life, into three separate Trusts, designated as the "Survivor's Trust," the "Marital Trust," and the "Residual Trust."

This subparagraph is followed by **13** other paragraphs which prescribe what the trustee is to do, concerning the three trusts. Nowhere is a name assignment made to any of the trusts. A trust is an entity which requires a distinguishing name of its own. This is crucially important when a trust becomes irrevocable (such as upon a trustor's death).

Typically, when a revocable living trust is initially drawn up, a name is assigned such as—

The Jones Family Living Trust (for joint trustors),
or,
The John Jones Living Trust (for a single trustor).

But when John Jones or Mary Jones dies, what is to be the name of each's irrevocable trust? Certainly, the words "family" and "living" would be omitted.

Using the nomenclature insisted on above, there could be the John J. Jones *Residual* Trust (or the Mary M. Jones Residual Trust). Here, the term "residual" implies that all applicable death tax accounting has been made. What's left over — the residual — is free of any further transfer taxing.

As to the "insisted on" survivor's trust and marital trust, we see no point in them. So long as the surviving trustor is alive, both said trusts are revocable. Any assets intended for them are includible in the surviving trustor's estate at the time of her demise. The transfer tax (gift or death) then applies. For probate avoidance purposes, the assets already are in the marital living trust.

If there is no name assigned to the trust, you, as trustee, should name the trust after the deceased trustor.

Article I: Example Styles

Inasmuch as most trust preparers are attorneys, they organize their work product into article form: Article I, Article II . . . Article

XV. This is the format in which the U.S. Constitution was written back in 1787. This practice continues today for legal documents and contracts. Although the Constitution is organized as preamble, article, section, clause, and paragraph, modern trust instruments short-change the preamble, sections, and clauses. They assign to each paragraph a two-decimal sequential numbering system, sometimes alpha-numeric, but most times numeric only. For example, the paragraphs under Article III frequently are numbered 3.01, 3.02, 3.03, etc. Sometimes the word "Article" is used; sometimes just the Roman numeral III. Sometimes the articles are titled and subtitled; sometimes not. Different styles — and different words and phrases — are used by different preparers.

To illustrate how trust writing styles differ, we present below three different versions of Article I. Each is extracted from existing active trust instruments. Article I tends to be a combination preamble and designation of the trust estate.

Example 1 —

All property subject to this instrument from time to time, including property listed in Exhibit A, is referred to as the "Trust Estate" and shall be held, administered, and distributed according to this instrument.

Example 2 —

The Trustors do hereby deliver and transfer to the Trustee the property described in Exhibit A (community property of husband and wife), Exhibit B (separate property of husband, if any), and Exhibit C (separate property of wife, if any) as attached hereto and made a part hereof, which shall constitute the Initial Trust Estate and shall be held, administered, and distributed by the Trustee as hereinafter set forth.

Example 3 —

The purpose of the Trust is to provide for the protection and management of the Trustors' assets during their joint lifetimes and to provide for the orderly disposition of the assets of the Trust upon the deaths of the Trustors without any supervision by the Court.

Property subject to this instrument listed in the Exhibit A attached and/or to which title is held in the name of the Trust or Trustee is referred to as the "Trust Estate" and shall be held, administered, and distributed in accordance with this instrument.

Altogether, Example 3 consisted of about 650 words of which we cite only 90 of those words. Thus, you can see that preparer styles can distract you from your primary role as a trustee. As to your primary role, all three examples use the exact same words, namely:

*The "Trust Estate" . . . **shall be held, administered, and distributed** . . . in accordance with this instrument.*

Always keep these key words in mind: "**shall be** — HELD, ADMINISTERED, and DISTRIBUTED . . .". The mandatory words get us back to the premise of Chapter 3: Legal Duties. As a trustee, you are to function as a conservator and distributor of the trust estate: **not** as an entrepreneurial empire builder. If you keep these words in mind, you'll be better able to sort through the wordiness and puffery, and get to the meat of your contract.

Disregard During-Life Provisions

Much of the puffery in a living trust originates from provisions directed to the trustor or trustors while alive. Because most trustors think "everything is taken care of" when they sign their Declaration of Trust, preparers often go out of their way to keep the trust viable, while one or both trustors are alive. This necessitates quite detailed instructions on self-administrative tasks in which the trustor acts as a trustee in his/her own behalf. As a result, many paragraphs contain the focus phrase: "during the lifetime of the trustor," or "during their joint lifetimes," or other phrases addressing a trustor (who is not mentally incompetent or physically incapacitated).

We haven't found a living trustor yet who reads and follows (to the letter) the preparer-inserted self-administrative instructions. Invariably, the trustor goes on with his/her/their usual way of doing business. The attitude of most living trustors is this: "I've been doing things this way all my life; I'm not going to change now. When I die, my trustee can take over."

Consequently, we suggest that you **disregard** all instructions to living trustors. As you skim-read and spot-check the trust instrument from page 1 through page 35 (or whatever), *check off* — delete — every paragraph which is addressed to a living trustor, whether single or joint. Using your photocopy of the trust document, "redline" these paragraphs out. All of these paragraphs are generally classed as **reserved powers** by the trust creator(s).

Why do we make our red-lining suggestion so confidently? Answer: Because of the stance that the IRS takes on all personal and family trusts. Any such trust in which *any person* has a reserved or reversionary interest which is exercisable while alive (other than a full-fledged trustee of an irrevocable trust) is deemed by the IRS to be a Grantor Type Trust. A "grantor" is any person — trustor, donor, spouse, or other person having an ownership interest in the trust estate — who conveys power to someone else to invade the trust for that person's own benefit.

As to grantor-type trusts, here's what the IRS has to say—

*A grantor type trust is a legal trust under applicable state law that is **not recognized** as a separate taxable entity for income tax purposes **because** the grantor or other substantial owners **have not relinquished complete dominion and control** over the trust property.* [Emphasis added.]

In other words, you can save yourself a lot of headaches if you disregard altogether those instructions for distributions of income or capital (corpus/principal) to a living trustor from his or her own trust-assigned property. It is not until a trustor relinquishes all dominion and control over said property that the trust is tax recognized. This occurs only after a trustor deceases.

The After-Death Paragraphs

There are certain particular portions of the trust instrument that you really want to concentrate on. These portions are those instructions on what to do after the death of the "first" trustor **and** after the death of the "second" trustor (in a spousal joint trust). The introductory wording to such paragraphs either reads or implies distributive intent—

Upon Death of Trustor
Upon Death of "First" Trustor
Upon Death of "Surviving" Trustor

The finding words and article numbering will differ, depending on the style and formality of the document preparer. For example, a 35-page active trust instrument of which we are aware, signifies the location of the after-death paragraphs as follows:

Article IV: Division and Distribution of Trust After Death of a Trustor

Article V: Administration of Trusts for Benefit of Surviving Trustor

Article VI: Administration and Distribution of Trusts After Death of Surviving Trustor

Together, Articles IV, V, and VI comprise approximately 3,500 words requiring 12 pages of text. Obviously, no one can memorize so many words. Therefore, it is necessary to read, reread, study, and digest the *essence* of the 12 pages.

In the above example, the essence is that upon the death of the first trustor, three trusts shall be created, namely: (A) Survivor's, (B) Marital, and (C) Residual [Article IV]. The surviving trustor has unlimited access to the income and capital of the survivor's trust, limited access to the marital trust, and "last-resort" access to the residual trust [Article V]. When the surviving trustor dies, the survivor's and marital trusts disappear. All asset leftovers from these two trusts dump into the residual trust for distribution to the successor named beneficiaries [Article VI]. Thus, in about 100 words, we've given you the essence of what 3,500 words in an A-B-C type trust instrument says. This is what we mean by "read, study, and digest" the after-death paragraphs. This kind of effort will give you a sense of direction.

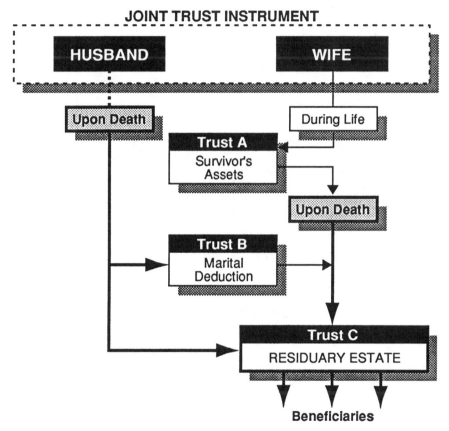

JOINT TRUST INSTRUMENT

Fig. 4.2 - Typical A-B-C Family Trust Plan

You need more than just a sense of direction, however, You need to prepare for yourself a little diagram or map, such as presented in Figure 4.2. From the origin of the trust estate when the spousal trustors are alive, you need to trace through what goes into, and out of, each of the A, B, and C trusts. Each trust serves a different function in conserving — and *consuming* — the marital estate throughout the remaining life of the surviving trustor. Having ourselves read the above-cited Articles IV, V, and VI at least three times, our depiction in Figure 4.2 gives you a working idea of how to approach dissecting and digesting what your trust administration activities are to be about. This is all part of what we call *trustee preparation* . . . before really taking charge.

Scope the Trust Estate

Once the decedent trustor's death tax affairs are out of the way, review all "documents and things" that prescribe the trust estate for ongoing administration. Technically, the trust estate comprises only those assets which are remnants of the decedent's estate, plus other additions which are expressly directed to be held under supervision by the trust instrument. In the classical A-B-C family trust, the first decedent's trust estate is Trust C: the residual trust.

More functionally, Trust C is referred to as the "Bypass Trust." This is because it bypasses the surviving trustor's estate when the trustor (the "second" spouse) deceases, and death tax accounting is resurrected all over again. The estate of each decedent trustor (whether a joint trust or not) has to run its own gauntlet of death taxation procedures.

Typical bypass language in an A-B-C trust goes something like this (as excerpted and slightly edited):

> *The Residual Trust shall consist of the balance of the Deceased Trustor's interest in the Trustor's community property, the balance of the Deceased Trustor's quasi-community property, the Deceased Trustor's separate property, . . . any additions from the decedent's Will or by life insurance policies on the decedent's life, . . . and any interest to other property disclaimed by the Surviving Spouse (such as in marital deduction property).*

These excerpts are sweep-type instructions. That is, you sweep into the residual/bypass trust all items of value that have gone, or will go, through the death tax and/or gift tax "sweeper." Thereafter, no further transfer taxes (gift/death) apply to the property items in said trust. To help you grasp better this sweep-in and bypass concept, we present Figure 4.3. Ordinarily, the first item swept in is the death tax exemption amount ($1,000,000 or so). This at least saves the surviving trustor from any worry of being taxed on her decedent spouse's exemption property. Amounts in excess of the exemption are either death taxed or gift taxed depending on events at the time of transfer into the bypass trust.

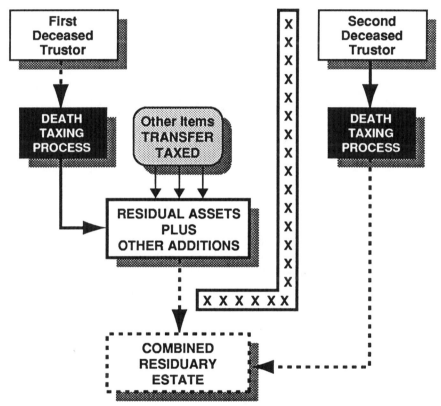

Fig. 4.3 - Concept of "Bypassing" Second Deceased Trustor's Estate

At this stage of our discussion, you simply gather and scope the nature and extent of the property intended for the bypass trust. To do this, you need to review all exhibits (specific property assignments) attached to the trust instrument, all amendments (changes in the sweep instructions), the decedent's will, life insurance on the decedent, the current decedent's Form 706 (Death Tax Return), any prior related trusts of which the decedent is a beneficiary, any gifts and disclaimers from related persons other than the surviving spouse, and any disclaimed interests in marital property by the surviving spouse. Your objective in this effort is to locate where the intended property is, and stake a claim to it. You are not yet ready to take it over and log it into the trust books of account. You still have a few other preparatory tasks.

Any Generational Skips?

There is one area of trust administration that will thoroughly confound you. It has to do with Generation-Skipping Transfers (GSTs). A GST is "skipping over" the child or children of the deceased trustor(s), and directing a corpus distribution from the trust to one or more grandchildren, great grandchildren, or great-greats. The skipping-over will severely impact your trust duties. When such distributions are directed, what was previously a simple residuary trust (all distributions of corpus going to the children of the trustors) now becomes a GST trust. When this happens a GST tax applies! This is another transfer tax (an **add-on**) similar to the gift/death tax imposed at time of a trustor's death.

The idea behind the GST tax is that, if the deceased trustor skips over his children, the children would pay no gift/death tax on the property transferred to their children (the trustor's grandchildren). Otherwise if the trust property went to the children (no skips) and they, in turn, transferred it to their children, a "second" (third, or fourth, etc.) transfer tax would apply to the same property that was gift/death taxed when it went into the residuary trust. Therefore, any generational skips deprive the IRS of federal death tax revenue. To compensate for this loss of revenue, a GST rate of 55% applies to all generational skips whose aggregate distributive value exceeds $1,000,000 (1 million). In most cases, GST provisions are seldom made for residuary trust estates of less than $3,000,000.

Obviously, your concern at this point is: Does the trust instrument provide for any generational skips? To find out, you need to locate and read through any distributive clauses that name grandchildren and great-grandchildren as skip beneficiaries while their parents are alive. If you find any bona fide generational skips, *highlight* the applicable clauses; you'll have to refer to them from time to time.

As a synopsis of the above, plus that which follows, we present Figure 4.4. The presentation is simply an outline of your extractive tasks that will help you avoid going back over 35 pages or so of trust documentation, repeatedly.

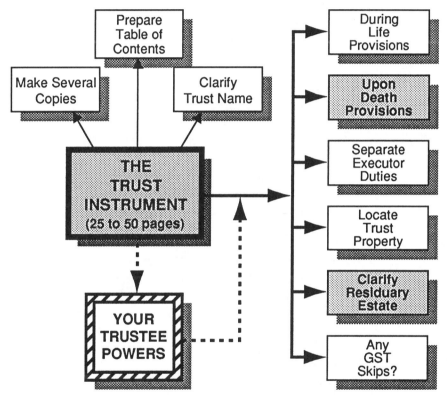

Fig. 4.4 - Preparatory Effort Before "Taking Charge" of Trust Property

Enshrine Your Powers

All trust instruments repeat the probate law of the state of domicile of the trustor, with respect to trustee powers. An appendix to the trust document displaying the state law could serve just as well. However, the instrument provides an opportunity to embellish on the powers as they expressly apply to the designated trust property and its beneficiaries.

Typically, a trustee's powers are enumerated in a separate article of their own. Said article may be titled: Trust Powers, General Trust Provisions, or General Trust Administrative Provisions. The introductory wording to the enumerated list goes as follows:

To carry out the provisions of any Trust created by this instrument, the Trustee shall have the following powers in addition to those powers now or hereafter conferred by law:

1. *Power to Retain Trust Property*
2. *Power to Manage Trust Property*
3. *Power to Invest and Reinvest Trust Assets*
4. *Power to Borrow and Encumber Trust Assets*
5. *Power to Participate in Reorganizations and Liquidations*
6. *Power to Vote Securities*
7. *Power to Pay Taxes Assessed Against the Trust*
8. *Power to Hold Undivided Interests*
9. *Power to Initiate Litigation or Settle Claims*
10. *Power to Lease*
11. *Power to Lend Money to Trustors' Probate Estates*
12. *Power to Employ Agents and Delegates*
13. *Power to Insure Trust Assets Against Loss*
14. *Power to Register Securities in Nominee Name*
15. *Power to Administer the Assets of Separate Trusts Without Physical Division*
16. *Power to Distribute in Kind*
17. *Power to Withhold Payment*
18. *Power to Release Powers*

Our suggestion is that you extract the enumerated powers from your trust instrument, and "enshrine" them on a 5"x 7" card (or other hardcopy product). Post the card or other product in the forepart of the books of account that you set up. This way, as you perform your duties you'll not need to refer to the trust contract . . . unless absolutely necessary.

5

GETTING DOWN TO BUSINESS

Once A Trustor Deceases, Any Income Of $600 Or More Per Year Generated By The Trust Property Is TAX ACCOUNTABLE. This Means Applying For A Trust ID, Opening A Bank Account, Rearranging The Property For Passive Income Production, And Registering All Communications With, And Distributions To, The Beneficiaries. Real Property Outstate Of The Domicile Of The Trustee Causes Endless Jurisdictional Problems With State Taxing Agencies. When A Trustor's Operating Business Is Assigned To The Trust, Decision Is Required On Whether Or Not To Continue It. A Trust Is Not A Long-Term Entrepreneurial Entity.

Managing the trust estate of a decedent is a business process of its own. Particularly so, because it is the decedent's money and property intended for beneficiaries who often are not the trustee thereof. Any business where your own money is not at stake requires *defensive* records and accounting that will withstand scrutiny upon demand. There are times — unforeseen — when a decedent's beneficiaries can be very demanding indeed. This is because it is "just natural" to suspect the trustee of wrongdoing,whatever may be the pretext.

Before a trustee can really settle down into his management duties, he needs to take a little time to organize his operation so that it does not overburden him. For one thing, since he is dealing with a separate entity — the residuary trust (which is irrevocable) — a separate **Tax ID** number is required. This requirement alone implies that one scrutinizing interest is the IRS (together with state and local taxing and regulatory interests). A trust **is a taxable entity** just like any other business enterprise. You should keep this point in focus at all times.

Certainly, you need to set up a separate bank account, a register of all designated beneficiaries, an inventory of trust assets, and tax basis adjustments for starting a whole new accounting on the income from, and transactions in, those assets. Think of your overall operation as a "fresh start" in a new business. The main difference is that you've been handed the remnants of an old business, but now you have to start de novo (once again; anew).

Our experience has been that most trustors do not organize their affairs with afterlife management and distribution in mind. They leave those matters to the trustee. In this chapter, therefore, we want to focus on the organizational tasks that you must go through in order to arrange your activities into an efficient and well-run operation. We want you to treat this chapter as a step-by-step checkoff list of things to do once the trust estate is known, and before any trust disributions are made.

Verify Payment of Transfer Taxes

No irrevocable trust estate is ready to start operation until all of the decedent's money and property have been inventoried and appraised by the executor thereof. Even then, technically, the property does not come within the purview of the trustee until all transfer taxes have been determined and paid. As the ongoing conservator and distributor of the trust property, you do not want to start off with any doubts about the status of transfer tax matters. Transfer taxation is a **priority lien** on all money and property that passes, or has passed, from a decedent's estate to his trust estate.

A "transfer tax" is strictly for the privilege of transferring money and property gratuitously. A gratuitous transfer is the transferring of property to family members and to other close persons, including trusts, without the recipients paying the transferor anything in return.

Gratuitous transfers are totally unlike everyday competitive business transactions. Said transactions involve the sale, exchange, abandonment, bankruptcy, foreclosure, and involuntary conversion of property. These business arrangements are called: "arm's-length" transfers. They are at arm's length because there is an exchange of money, property, services, or debt relief between unrelated parties under changing market conditions. Obviously, transfers into personal trusts do not involve competitive pricing and market conditions. It is for this reason that a transfer tax applies.

There are three forms of transfer tax. There is a gift tax (on living donors and trustors); there is a death tax (on deceased persons, whether trustor or not); and there is a GST tax (for generation-skipping, whether the transferor is alive or dead). The whole purpose of the gift/death/GST tax is to equate gratuitous transfers to *full and adequate consideration* as though they were competitive arm's-length transactions. Inadequate or deficient transfer tax accounting clouds the title of money and property assigned to the trust. It also clouds its acceptance value for tax basis and other starting-the-books accounting purposes.

Satisfaction of the transfer taxation process is evidenced by the following two federal tax returns, namely:

> **Form 709**: *U.S. Gift (and Generation-Skipping Transfer) Tax Return.*
>
> **Form 706**: *U.S. Estate (and Generation-Skipping Transfer) Tax Return.*

As a trustee, you MUST procure a copy of each of these returns in which your decedent's trust is designated as a recipient of money or property. On the face of each return, there is a sequence of tax computations and exemptions that applies. You want not only a signed, filed copy of each return, but also a photocopy of the written check(s) or electronic transfer(s) of tax payments actually made. You want hardcopy evidence that these matters have indeed been taken care of. Do not accept hearsay statements or other assurances.

As a trustee, you are not responsible for preparing the gift, death, and GST returns (Forms 709 and 706 above). This is the responsibility of the transferor, whoever that might be. This would be the donor while alive (*any* donor), the trustor while alive, and the executor of the estate of a deceased person (*any* person). Your job is to satisfy yourself that the proper transfer tax returns have been prepared and timely filed. It is your duty to see that all property irrevocably assigned to the trust starts off with a clean tax slate. As you'll see in subsequent chapters, you will have enough tax accounting chores of your own to do . . . to keep you busy.

Apply for Trust Tax ID

Once you are satisfied that the transfer tax returns (Forms 709 and 706) have been filed, you can start your first chore for setting up the trust operation. The task is to apply to the IRS for a Tax ID number for the residuary trust. You make the application on **Form SS-4**: *Application for Employer Identification Number*. The trust may not actually have any employees, yet the SS-4 is still the proper form to use.

Where do you get Form SS-4?

Answer: From the IRS, of course. You can visit the IRS's Internet Web Site, or you can check your phone directory for federal tax forms. Request the form itself *plus* its three pages of instructions. The instructions will step you through the 20 lines or so of information required. The instructions will also tell you that you can apply for the trust ID by telephone. However, you can do this only after you have the SS-4 completed and by your side . . . ready to be faxed to the IRS.

Obviously, make application in the name of the trust, such as THE JOHN J. JONES TRUST. Clearly indicate that you are the trustee and that John Jones was indeed the trustor (now deceased). Check the box where it asks: *Type of entity* ☒ Trust. Also, check the box which asks: *Reason for applying* ☒ *Created a trust* (specify type). Use caution when specifying the type of trust. The instructions tell you not to use Form SS-4 for a revocable trust. So, make sure the word "irrevocable" is entered.

Particular caution is required when making an entry on the line designated as: *Date business started or acquired (Mo., day, year)*. This is the date that you take over — or expect to take over — the trust property and for which you are tax responsible from such date forward. It is **not** the date that the attorney prepared and notarized the trust instrument. Nor is it the date of death of the deceased trustor. It is the date you anticipate that you will have all books of account set up . . . ready to start the trust activities. Pick a date that is realistic; one which allows the executor adequate time to complete his tasks, before you take over.

The next entry to be aware of is: *Closing month of accounting year*. The instructions say—

Generally, a trust must adopt a calendar year.

This means that you enter "12" for 12th month, or December. It could be that your starting date would cause your first accounting year to be a "short year" (less than 12 months). This is O.K.

When Form SS-4 is approved, a 9-digit "account number" is assigned. The instructions accompanying the written approval tell you to use the ID number on all tax forms and all communications with the IRS concerning trust activities. You'll receive preprinted instructions to this effect on a form titled: *Notice of New Employer Identification Number Assigned.*

Open Checking-Only Account

Your next task is to open a checking account with a local bank or other depository institution in the name of the trust. You want this to be a checking-only account: noninterest bearing. Most interest-bearing checking accounts pay only around 2% interest per annum. Keeping track of this rate of interest as income is a tax nuisance. Especially since our recommendation is that you keep a "rolling average" balance that is minimal.

To appreciate the nuisance effect of a 2% rate of interest, consider a rolling average balance of $10,000 for the entire year. This would be taxable income in the amount of $200 (10,000 x 0.02). For comparison purposes, suppose the trust estate amounted to $1,000,000 and that it earned a modest 6% rate of return. The trust estate income would be $60,000 (1,000,000 x 0.06). The bank interest income would represent just 1/3 of 1% (200 ÷ 60,000). It just doesn't make sense to complicate the management of a $1,000,000 trust estate for an amount of interest income this low.

Your ability to decide on a checking-only account versus an interest-bearing account is the first test of your ability to make down-to-earth practical decisions. Open the account in the name of the trust, with your name as trustee. For example, the account could be designated as—

THE JOHN J. JONES TRUST

DOREEN SMITH, Trustee

On the signature withdrawal card, show your name and signature. In addition, add the name of a *successor trustee* (with his or her signature) whom the trustor has appointed or instructed you to appoint. This way, should you be unable to serve as a trustee for any reason, the successor trustee would have access to the account.

As to the initial deposit, draw from your own checking or savings account and deposit $100 into the trust account. On your records, show the $100 as a loan advanced by you to the trust. You simply want to get the account opened and funded so that the bank or other institution can print up your first supply of blank checks. You can get your $100 back later.

As a general guideline, set an average balance goal of approximately $10,000. You want to keep enough in the account to pay all operating expenses of the trust at the end of each month. All monetary receipts and transfers due the trust are deposited into this one account only. When the account balance exceeds $10,000, sweep the entire excess into a money market investment account (which we'll get to shortly).

Collect All Monetary Assets

With the trust checking account opened, you are now in a position to contact all account holders of monetary assets. A "monetary asset" has a unit value of $1. That is, it neither appreciates nor depreciates over time. It has a fixed face value. Monetary assets consist of bank accounts, savings accounts, money market accounts, certificates of deposit, trust deeds, promissory notes, installment sale contracts, judgment awards, life insurance, and the like. If any of these items are intended for the trust, you must contact all holders thereof.

This assumes, of course, that you know who the account holders are, or at least you can find out. You can start with the executor of the deceased trustor's estate. Or, you can rummage through all papers and files left behind by the decedent. You are looking for names and addresses of monetary account holders, and the latest posted balances in said accounts.

Inform each account holder that you are the duly appointed trustee, and that you request that the outstanding dollar balances be forwarded to you. In every case, the holder would want a certified copy of the trustor's death certificate and a verified copy of the pages of the trust instrument designating you as the trustee (together with the signature and notarization pages thereto). Prepare these documents and attach them to your formal request (demand) letter. Instruct each addressee to make out a check payable to the name of the trust and forward it to you. Make each initial contact in writing by certified mail.

In all likelihood, most account holders will not immediately respond to your collection request. They will respond to your letter, but not with a check payable. Particularly those accounts located outstate; they will want some kind of "court document" describing the account and directing that it be turned over to you. To these account holders, the trust instrument carries little or no weight. This leaves you little choice but to petition the probate court for an order directing that the account be turned over to you. Procuring such an order adds delay.

Instate account holders will probably send you preprinted legal forms of their own. You'll be instructed to complete their forms and get your signature notarized. Usually, these account holders respond with a check in a reasonable time.

The idea is to strip all account holders of monetary balances intended for the trust. When received, deposit each check into the trust's checking account. This gives you a "capital cushion" to start the trust activities with adequate money on hand.

Spend your early days collecting all money due, before worrying about collecting any property due the trust. Expect some difficulty collecting full balances on debt obligations such as trust deeds, promissory notes, judgment awards, installment sales, etc. Unless a debt instrument has an "acceleration clause" in it (full payment for cause), you may not be able to collect the unpaid balance until the contractual maturity date.

Open Investment Account

As the money collections come in, start thinking about opening a *money market* investment account in the trust's name. Contact a financial institution of your choice. Choose one which offers *check-writing privileges* with their money market accounts. Get the best rate of interest and most convenient withdrawal privileges that you can. You want to transfer into this account all monies from the checking-only account that exceed your target average balance needed for trust operational purposes.

Limit withdrawals from the money market account to purchases of other investments and to distributions to beneficiaries. This is to be strictly an investment account: **not** an operating account. Money going from this account to the beneficiaries is also a form of investment.

The kind of arrangement we have in mind for the working account and the investment account is presented in Figure 5.1. With this depiction in mind, we urge that all receipts due the trust be deposited in the working account only. Do not short-cut the process by making some deposits directly into the investment account. Always go through the working account first, then transfer to the investment account. Always transfer in even $1,000 amounts. This way, every dollar coming into the trust is third-party traceable. Disciplining yourself along the lines of Figure 5.1 will stand you well, when someday challenged to account for all monies.

If you expect the amount of investment money available on any single day to exceed $100,000, we urge a tax-free type of money market account. Talk to your mutual fund, brokerage firm, or financial institution about their tax-free money market options. Believe us, when making distributions to beneficiaries, if you can tell them that part of the distribution is "tax free," they'll bless you.

Whether you get a tax-free or taxable interest earnings rate, make sure you get a money market investment account. At this stage of your takeover of trust assets you are not ready to jump into any variable-unit investments (stocks, bonds, mutual funds, partnerships, S corporations, real estate mortgage interest conduits, private shares, and so on). Treat this fixed-unit investment account as a "parking place" for excess trust money until you've had more time to study and weigh better investment options.

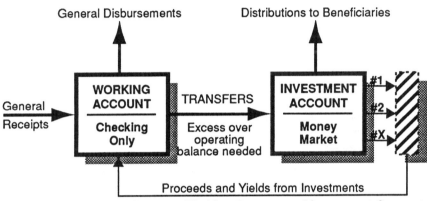

Fig. 5.1 - Relationship Between Working Account and Investment Account

Plan Property Rearrangement

Unless the deceased trustor had the foresight and advice to streamline and simplify his property holdings, you'll be left with a lot of clutter and complexity. Most trustors spend a lifetime accumulating their wealth through stock portfolios, mutual funds, mortgage notes, installment contracts, collectibles (coins, works of art, antiques), real estate (residential, commercial, farming), emerging businesses (partnerships, etc.), vehicles (cars, boats, campers), and other assorted property items (horses, rare animals, guns, trophies) which constitute their "investment" in their future. Part of the future that they did not consider is the management of these items after their demise.

As we pointed out previously, it is better that you be responsible for a few good property holdings, rather than for a diverse multiplicity of good and not-so-good holdings. Too many properties to manage exposes you to higher chances of errors and omissions in some important duties. Our position is, therefore, that you need to liquidate some properties (convert them to money), auction off other items to the highest bidder, and rearrange others into a long-term income-producing "machine." In other words, you need to prepare a *property rearrangement plan*.

To prepare such a plan, take a detailed inventory of all property items that are intended for the trust estate. Segregate the items into the following categories:

1. Marketable Securities
   — stocks, bonds, mutual funds

2. Quasi-Marketable Instruments
   — second deeds of trust, mortgage notes, personal loans, installment sales, accounts receivable

3. Collectibles of Value
   — precious stones, coins, and jewelry; works of art, sculptures, paintings, antiques

4. Vehicles, Animals, & Equipment
   — whatever is fair marketable

5. Ownership of Existing Businesses
   — proprietorships, partnerships, small corporations

6. Real Estate
   — in every conceivable form: pristine land, mountain tops, wet land, timber land, natural resources, oil wells, lake fronts, ocean fronts, easements, rights of way, etc.

As much as possible, physically inspect each property item on your own. Inform each current holder or custodian that, as trustee, you intend to claim the property when "all paper work" is executed. During the physical inspection process, decide which items you want to keep and which you want to get rid of.

As a general guide for your rearrangement plan, think in terms of *no more than—*

- Three readily marketable security issues
- Three readily rentable real estate parcels
- One reasonably profitable ongoing business

. . . plus all the cash money that you can muster.

All items (other than money) selected for retention or acquisition should be income producing. As a rule of thumb, use a conservative rate of return, such as 5% per annum. This should be the *net* return on the fair market value of the property held. Or, use the taxable rate of return on the trust's money market account as your decision guide whether to keep, sell, or buy.

For example, suppose the trust has, or would like to acquire, a parcel of rental real estate valued at $200,000. If the going rent for that property is $1,000 per month, the gross rate of return would be 6% [(1,000/mo x 12 mo) ÷ 200,000]. Suppose the operating expenses (property taxes, insurance, repairs, utilities, etc.) averaged $350 per month. The net rate of return would be 3.9% [(12,000 − (350 x 12)) ÷ 200,000]. With these numbers, ask yourself this question: If I can sell the property for $200,000 and put the proceeds into a money market account earning 5% (with no management on my part), why should I struggle with all the headaches of being a landlord to net earn 3.9%?

Register Beneficiaries & Preferences

Just prior to taking complete control of all trust property, set up a register of all beneficiaries. (If there are only one or two beneficiaries, there is no need to do this.) For each beneficiary, enter name, address, phone number, age, and relationship to the deceased trustor(s). The idea is to keep a running log of all contacts with the beneficiaries: what they said, what they want, and what they complain about (if at all). Count on it: at some point along the way, you may be challenged concerning your performance of duties. If not directly by a beneficiary, then indirectly by a nosy family member, friend, or advisor of a beneficiary. The greater the value of the trust estate, the greater the likelihood of challenge therewith.

Your first "official" contact with each beneficiary should be in the form of a well-thought-out letter. Inform each addressee that you are the duly appointed trustee (even if such is already known), and that you have certain discretionary powers over all trust property. Indicate that your powers are enumerated on pages xx through yy of that certain trust instrument dated _____. Then enclose a listing of the various items of trust property that you have inventoried and personally inspected.

Referring to the inventory, explain that you are in the process of taking management control over all of it. As you do so, state clearly that you intend to reduce the number of items to three to five substantial holdings. Explain that you will retain those income-producing and potentially appreciating properties which yield a return of 5% or more per year. You intend to liquidate all others for the best price you can get.

How you rearrange the property and manage it is your affair. But, you are open to comments, suggestions, and preferences from the beneficiaries. Keep all written replies and fax replies on file (in the registry). As to telephone replies, make brief though accurate entries of your own. The purpose of the registry is to have a source of reference on all *communications* with — and *distributions* to — each beneficiary. Our Figure 5.2 is a depiction of the general scheme we have in mind.

Liquefy and Rearrange

After notifying the beneficiaries of your liquidation and rearrangement plan, start doing it! Issue a formal request/demand to all holders of the trustor's property to transfer it to you. Your goal is to take legal possession by whatever means is required. Procedures will vary depending on the nature of the property, where it is located, and who the holder may be.

Almost every holder will require a written application for transfer, a copy of the death certificate, an abbreviated copy of the trust instrument, and — in some cases — a probate court order directing that the property be turned over to you. None of this will be straightforward. Figure somewhere between 30 to 90 days to corral all trust-designated property under your supervision.

Once you have one or more properties under your supervision, start contacting various sales agents, brokers, and auction houses in

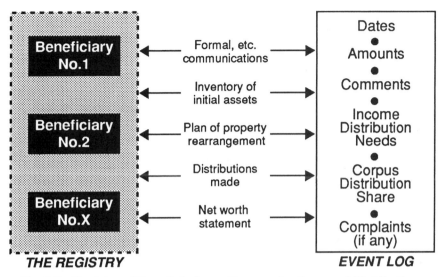

Fig. 5.2 - Registry of Beneficiaries re Communications and Distributions

the vicinity where each item is located. For those properties you do not intend to keep in the trust, sign listing contracts to get them sold. Even properties you'd like to keep, if they are located outstate, list them for sale with a reputable dealer.

In the meantime, all items sold will have a *tax basis*, in reference to which the net proceeds from each sale will represent capital gain, return of capital, or capital loss. While you do not have to figure the gain or loss at time of sale, you will have to do so when the trust's accounting year ends. The important point here is that you need to establish a tax basis for each item sold.

How do you establish tax basis when a decedent's property is sold? Answer: You get most of the information from **Form 706**: *U.S. Estate Tax Return*. For real estate, the basis values will be shown in Schedule A; stocks and bonds on Schedule B; mortgages and notes on Schedule C; and other items on Schedules D, E, and F. If there were any gift transfers to the trust after the trustor's death, the "donor's adjusted basis" is entered on Schedule A of **Form 709**: *U.S. Gift Tax Return*. Extracting tax basis data from these two forms often requires separate analysis and computation. As a consequence, you must retain in your possession a copy of each Form 706 and Form 709 that is pertinent to the trust. When the time comes to prepare *income* tax returns for the trust, the tax basis returns will be crucial.

Dispose of Outstate Property

As the trustee, the trust is deemed to be domiciled in the state where **you** reside. It is not domiciled in the state where the trustor lived, nor in the state where he deceased. There are tax administrative reasons for this. The trustee is responsible for all income taxation — federal *and* state — against the trust property. It follows, therefore, that the jurisdiction for enforceability of filing trust income tax returns is the domicile of the trustee.

In addition, all states assert jurisdiction over tangible and real property located within their borders. Whenever income is produced from such property, whether held or sold, the owners must file an income tax return, both federal and state. In nine states of the U.S. 50, no state income tax is imposed. [The nine states are Alaska, Florida, Nevada, New Hampshire, South Dakota, Tennessee, Texas, Washington, and Wyoming.] Thus, in 41 states, income taxes apply to tangible and real trust property located in those states. This is **not** the case, however, for *intangible* property (bank accounts, mutual funds, brokerage accounts, etc.) due to mutually reciprocal agreements.

Unfortunately, if the trust has tangible or real property in a nontaxing state, and the trustee resides in a taxing state, the trustee's state will tax the income from property in the nontaxing state. The situation worsens if property is located in a taxing state when the trustee resides in a nontaxing state. The trustee has to file a nonresident return with the taxing state. Matters can become maddening when property, especially real estate, is located in two or more jurisdictions outstate of the domicile of the trustee. As we try to depict in Figure 5.3, each state winds up taxing the taxes of the other state. Where real property is concerned, there is very little tax credit reciprocity among the states.

If the trust holds outstate property (*other than* financial accounts), our suggestion is that you dispose of that property as expeditiously as you can. List it with a reputable agent . . . and sell it! Because of the way the trust acquires ownership of property, the

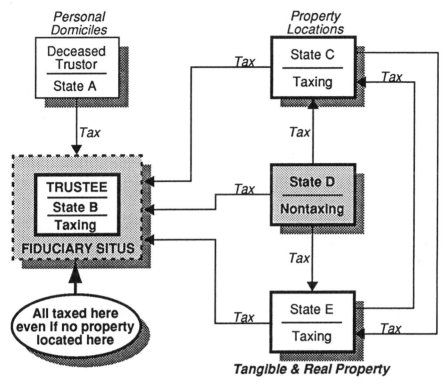

Fig. 5.3 - Jurisdictional Complexity with Outstate Property and Domiciles

trust gets a stepped-up tax basis to the property's fair market value at time of death of the trustor. Consequently, any taxable gain is likely to be negligible. If the income need after sale persists, you can replace the property with its instate equivalent.

When to Use Caution

As to the trust property, most of what we've touched on above relates to passive activities: portfolio investments and rental real estate. These activities do not require day-to-day attention nor frequent contact with customers. As a trustee, rarely would such activities require once-a-week attention; mostly it would be once-a-month. In contrast, an active business — proprietorship, partnership, or corporation — requires managerial attention daily. If property assigned to the trust by the trustor does not already consist of an active business, we think it is inadvisable to start one with the trust as the owner.

If the trustor was the owner or part-owner of an active business, you have some hard decisions to make. Do you continue the business? Do you sell it? Or, do you lease it to someone else or to some entity to run? Are there any beneficiaries who are already active participants in the business . . . or would like to be?

Whatever you do, you must use caution. Especially if you yourself have had little experience in managing a business on a daily basis. Even if you have had ample experience, we offer some guidelines that may help in your decision making.

One: Was the trustor a less than 10% owner? If so, to what extent was the trustor's capital (now, the trust's capital) essential to the operating success of the business? Are there any co-owners willing to buy the trust's interest? If not, would the business itself buy the trust's interest? If not, either sell to an outside interest or insist on redeeming the trust's share. A minority interest of less than 10% in a business has little impact on its management and success. It is best to get out.

Two: Was the trustor a less than 50% owner, but more than 10%? If so, was the trustor an active participant in the business? Even if so, can the business carry on without him? If the business can run without the trustor — and, therefore, without you as trustee — what kind of return on capital is the business generating? If the return is more than 10% per annum, stay with it. Stay a less than 50% owner as long as the majority interests will allow you to do so.

Three: Was the trustor a majority owner holding a more than 50% interest? If so, it is unlikely that the business could continue operation without your active participation. As a trustee, we think you would have a conflict of interest here. All closely-held businesses tend to be cash short; there would be temptation on your part to "borrow" needed operating funds from other property interests of the trust. Unless you can find a family member, close personal friend, or a competent beneficiary of the trustor to hire as manager, the business should be sold. Selling an active business takes much more time and finesse than selling a parcel of real estate.

Stabilize Your Modus Operandi

The premise throughout this book is that an irrevocable trust will continue in operation for several years or more. As the trustee thereof, you want to settle down and stabilize the number and types of property holdings that you will manage. To do so prudently, you want to have a "strategic spread" of property holdings. The target of the spread should be a combination of properties which provide (a) capital preservation, (b) income generation, and (c) capital growth potential. No one combination of properties is ideal. You'll have to try for that combination that works best for you.

Much depends on the amount of personal interest, time, and participation you want to devote to the trust business. You are not a broker; so don't wheel and deal on a daily or weekly regular basis. You are not an entrepreneur either. So don't try to build a corporate empire with the trust assets. You are a trustee only. This means that your primary role is to conserve and distribute the trust income and capital, and, ultimately, terminate the trust.

To help you achieve the strategic spread that you need, we offer what we call the "5-asset spread plan." That is, you should limit the property holdings to five *classes*, namely:

1. A money market investment account
    — interest earning: tax-free or taxable (your choice)

2. An income-equity portfolio of established corporate stock (or mutual fund account)
    — dividend earning: modest capital gain

3. A growth-income portfolio of "emerging" corporate entities: national and international
    — good capital gains: modest dividends

4. A "mix" of no more than three separate rental properties
    — residential, commercial, or industrial

— current income production with good capital appreciation potential

5. *Either* an operating small business with an established product line and customer base, *or* a "collection" of such items as rare coins, guns, stamps, works of art, antiques, Chinese porcelain, restored autos, etc.
— occasional sales with annual appreciation at least 5% over the CPI inflation rate

The idea above is to home in on a 5-property-class strategy and stick to it as your modus operandi. Within each class, if a chosen item is disappointing "rotate" it out . . . and rotate a replacement in. All along the way, keep culling out the poor performers. You can always transfer the proceeds from the checking-only working account to the Class 1 (money market) account and still earn a respectable rate of interest. Perhaps you can better visualize our postulated arrangement with Figure 5.4.

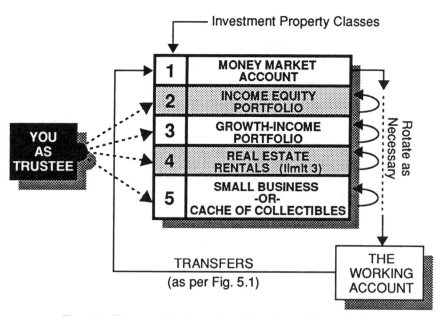

Fig. 5.4 - Example Strategy for Allocation of Trust Assets

Set Up Books of Account

No matter what your property arrangement for the trust assets may be, there is one duty that you cannot escape. If the trust property generates so much as $600 or more of *gross income* per year, an annual accounting to the IRS has to be made. The term "gross income" includes interest, dividends, rents, royalties, business income, farm income, capital gains, capital losses . . . whatever. It could well be that the trust operating expenses and distribution deductions reduce the taxable income to zero. Nevertheless, a yearly income tax return (Form 1041) still has to be filed. (We'll introduce you to Form 1041 in the next chapter.)

Even if the trust has no taxable income of its own, there are distributions and an accounting to be made to the beneficiaries. When distributions are made, there has to be a distinction between income (which is tax accountable by each beneficiary to the IRS) and corpus (return of capital to beneficiaries, which is *not* taxable). There also needs to be some end-of-the-year net worth statement made to the beneficiaries. The net worth statement gives them an idea of how much corpus is remaining in the trust for distribution later . . . or for consumption when the need is dire.

All such reportings, and others, require the setting up of adequate books of account. No prescribed format is required, so long as the books are posted regularly. This means that you can design your own format(s), purchase traditional style account books, or acquire (or download) computer programmed spread sheets. In our view, you need three separate sets of books, as follows:

A. Receipts and Disbursements

— For cash flow tracking of all receipts into and all disbursements out of the trust. As long as timely descriptive annotations are made on the checkbook stubs, the checking-only working account serves this vital recordkeeping function.

B. Income and Expenses

— For tax purposes accounting of the trust operation. Requires that both income and expenses be *segregated* into tax recognized categories for separate line entries on Form 1041 and its attached schedules.

C. Assets and Liabilities

— For beginning/ending net worth changes in trust corpus. Though not required for tax reasons, is required for legal reasons. End of year book values and market values should be shown.

On your one hand, it is simply "good business" to keep books and records on the management of trust property. On your other hand, it is good defensive strategy against challenges and disputes that may adversarially arise. Also, you need cumulative good records when the time comes to terminate the trust. And in the woodwork, as always, there is the IRS — and, possibly, some covetous attorney — keeping a watchful eye on you.

6

INTRODUCTION TO FORM 1041

When Property Is Assigned Irrevocably To A Trust, It Is Expected To Generate Income. When $600 Or More, Form 1041 Is Required. For Simple Trusts, ALL Net Positive Income Is Distributed To Living Beneficiaries . . . Who Pay The Tax Proportionately On Their Own Forms 1040. The 1041 Exemptions And Tax Rates Are Intentionally Designed To Encourage DISTRIBUTIION OF INCOME Currently. When Income Or Corpus Are Set Aside For Special Needs And/Or For Charities, The Trust Becomes "Complex." Then, Complex Taxation Rules Apply. If Any "Personal Service" Income Is Assigned To The Trust, Form 1041 Becomes Invalid.

As a trustee, there is one income tax form with which you MUST become familiar. You need not actually prepare it yourself — you can always engage a professional preparer — but you should know what it is about and why it exists. The particular form we have in mind is **Form 1041:** *U.S. Income Tax Return for Estates and Trusts.* Note that it applies to "Estates" as well as to trusts. This dual use causes some confusion. This is because two separate returns are involved. The Estate 1041 starts and ends at a different time, and for a different purpose, than does a Trust 1041.

To clarify the situation, it is useful to think of Form 1041 as a **sequel** to Form 1040. You surely already know about Form 1040: *U.S. Individual Income Tax Return.* The 1040 is for living persons only. The 1041 is for deceased persons and their trusts. The Estate 1041 starts on the date of death of a person, and continues until his (or her) estate is settled. An estate is "settled" when all transfer (gift/death/GST) taxes have been paid, and when the residuary property is distributed either directly to beneficiaries or assigned to a trust. Recall our "suspension period" message in Figure 1.5. The Trust 1041 starts thereafter and continues until the trust terminates.

If a trust generates so much as $600 in gross income in a calendar year, OR if it has a beneficiary who is a nonresident alien (regardless of gross income of the trust), Form 1041 is required. Therefore, it behooves us (in this chapter) to give you a general overview of the 1041, and how it differs from a 1040. We particularly want to explain the head portion of Form 1041 and the instructions the IRS issues with respect to it. We will identify a number of the schedules that go with the 1041, but will not detail them until it is instructively more appropriate. There is an "Other Information" part of Form 1041 (at the bottom of its page 2) which you will find enlightening.

Head Portion of Form 1041

The quickest way to sink your teeth into Form 1041 is for us to introduce and present its head portion. When we do this, you'll note an immediate difference between Forms 1040 and 1041. The 1041 headmatter is much less self-explanatory than the corresponding head portion of 1040. A glance at Figure 6.1 will tell you why.

Except for the trust name and trustee's address block, all other head portion blocks are referenced with a capital letter designation: A through G. Do not confuse these cap-letter designations with similar letters for Schedules A through K associated with the 1041. The headmatter designations are for referencing Specific Instructions that are found in the general instructions to Form 1041. Incidentally, you should make an effort to obtain a copy of the official Form 1041, its schedules, and its 27 pages of instructions. Check your phone directory and call the nearest IRS Forms Center. Or, you can try visiting the IRS's Internet Web Site.

Although we showed the headmatter blocks in Figure 6.1, we recap them here because of their importance. In alphabetical sequence, the headblocks (as officially titled) are:

FORM 1041	U.S. INCOME TAX RETURN for ESTATES & TRUSTS	Year

A Type of Entity

☐ Decedent's estate
☐ Simple trust
☐ Complex trust
☐ Grantor trust
☐ Bankruptcy estate
☐ Pooled income fund

Name of Trust:

(If grantor trust, see instructions)

Name of Fiduciary:

Street or P.O. Box Address:

City, State, & ZIP:

C Entity EIN Number

D Date Entity Created

E Nonexempt charitable and split-interest trusts

☐ Sec. 4947 (a)(1)
☐ Not a private foundation
☐ Sec. 4947 (a)(2)

B Number of Schedules K-1 attached ▶

F Check applicable boxes

☐ Initial return
☐ Final return
☐ Amended return

Change in Fiduciary's ▶ ☐ Name ☐ Address

G Pooled mortgage account

☐ Bought
☐ Sold

Date

Fig. 6.1 - The Head Portion of Form 1041 for Family Trusts

A — Type of entity
B — Number of Schedules K-1
C — Employer identification number
D — Date entity created
E — Nonexempt charitable and split-interest trusts
F — Check applicable boxes
G — Pooled mortgage account

We'll skip Block A for the moment, and quickly run through blocks B through G.

Block B is simply a space for entering the number of beneficiaries of the trust. Each must receive separately a Schedule K-1. Block C is the Tax ID number that you applied for using Form SS-4 (discussed in Chapter 5). Block D is date that the trust took possession of all trust-assigned property and started earning income. (This was also discussed in Chapter 5.)

Block E, usually, is inapplicable to family trusts. Block E is for those highly funded trusts ($100,000,000 or more), which are partly charitable, partly noncharitable, and partly private foundation types. Special excise taxes apply for political expenditures, excess business holdings, jeopardizing charitable purposes, undistributed income, and other self-dealings under an arrangement for being a charitable remainder entity. These are committee-type entities, the trustees of which are unlikely to be reading this book. In your case, leave this block blank.

Block F: Initial return ☐ Final return ☐ or Amended return ☐. Check the appropriate box when applicable. Certainly, the first time you file a Trust 1041 return, you must check the "Initial" box.

Block G applies only if the trust bought or sold "certificates of participation" in Federal National Mortgage Association trusts. Such FNMA trusts themselves are tax exempt, but any earnings from your participation in them are not tax exempt.

Type of Entity Checkboxes

Block A in Figure 6.1 lists six separate checkboxes under the item: Type of Entity. With some quick comments, we can eliminate three of the six checkboxes. Elimination derives from the IRS instructions which say—

Check the appropriate box that describes the entity for which you [the fiduciary of the trust] *are filing the return.*

The implication is that you can check only one box for each tax year.

This gets us back to an earlier premise that you cannot have both an Estate 1041 and a Trust 1041 at the same time. A *decedent's estate* and a decedent's *trust* are separate tax accountable entities. Since we are focusing only on trusts in this book, we can immediately eliminate the first checkbox in Block A: Decedent's Estate.

Two other checkboxes can also be eliminated quickly: Bankruptcy Estate and Pooled Income Fund. Only individuals and corporations can file for bankruptcy: trusts cannot. A trust doesn't go bankrupt; it terminates. A pooled income fund is a charitable remainder trust where the charity itself is the trustee of the trust property. Such trust can accept property from multiple unrelated donors. Professional trustees (working full time) are engaged to administer the "split-interests" of the charity and the life estate of each donor. This is not the kind of trust intended for this book.

We can also rule out *grantor type* trusts from our discussion, though not so quickly. In the IRS's words—

> *A grantor type trust is a legal trust under applicable state law that is **not recognized** as a separate taxable entity for income tax purposes **because** the grantor or other substantial owners **have not relinquished complete dominion and control** over the trust.* [Emphasis added.]

Ordinarily, a trustor/grantor relinquishes complete dominion and control over trust property only *after* he dies. However, complete relinquishment can apply to clearly *irrevocable portions* of the trust property, if specifically so designated. Otherwise, the "grantor trust" concept is a generic term that rules out virtually all variants of revocable and reversionary trusts created after March 1, 1986. This rule-out includes versions of so-called Family Estate Trusts which are promotionally identified as "pure," "equity," "prime," "funeral," "rabbi," or "constitutional" trusts.

As to all forms of grantor trusts, the 1041 instructions say—

> *Do not report on Form 1041 the income that is taxable to the grantor or another person . . .**who retains a more than 5% interest in any portion** of a trust. Report on Form 1041* [only] *that part of the income that is taxable to the trust.* [Emphasis added.]

These instructions infer that grantor trusts are split-interest trusts. That is, all revocable/reversionary parts go on Form 1040, whereas only the irrevocable part goes on Form 1041.

Needless to say, determining which part is revocable and which part is irrevocable adds complexity to trust administration. Furthermore, as trustee, you must become expert in the 10 grantor trust rules prescribed by IRC Sections 671 through 678: ***Persons Treated as Substantial Owners***. In short, therefore, grantor type trusts are beyond the focus of this book.

The above eliminations leave only two remaining likely checkboxes in Block A of Form 1041. These two are:

☐ Simple trust, OR ☐ Complex trust.

We need to discuss these two types in some detail.

Simple vs. Complex Trusts

The term "simple" or "complex" as applied to Trust 1041s describes their tax distinctions only. The distinction depends on what the trust instrument directs the trustee to do. Both trust forms are irrevocable; the distinction is how and when the income and corpus are distributed.

On this point, the 1041 instructions say—

A trust may qualify as a simple trust if:

1. The trust instrument requires that all income be distributed currently;

2. The trust instrument does not provide that any amounts are to be paid, permanently set aside, or used for charitable purposes; and

3. The trust does not distribute amounts allocated to the corpus of the trust.

On the subject of complex trusts, the 1041 instructions say—

A complex trust is any trust that does not qualify as a simple trust as explained above.

Thus, a complex trust is simpler in concept than a simple trust. Sounds weird, doesn't it?

The IRS computer knows the difference. Therefore, do not casually check the "complex trust" box out of misunderstanding whether you qualify as a simple trust or not. In a complex trust, the IRS computer is looking for the following "accumulation reports":

Schedule J — Accumulation Distribution for a Complex Trust;
Form 1041A — Trust Accumulation of Charitable Amounts; and
Form 4970 — Tax on Accumulation Distribution of Trusts.

Believe us. These reports are indeed complex.

Complex trusts rely on the accumulation of distributions remaining in the trust, thereby softening the tax impact to beneficiaries. When there are set-asides for charities, very complex throwback and allocation rules come into play. When in doubt, always check ☐ *Simple trust*. If this turns out to be wrong, you can amend the return later (by so signifying in Block F).

There is one dominant distinguishing feature of a simple trust. It is the requirement that all current income be distributed to designated beneficiaries. The term "current" means at least once annually. The term "all income" does not mean all gross income; it means all *taxable* income. By distributing all taxable income of the trust to the beneficiaries, they pay the tax. The trust nets out with zero taxable income, and therefore zero tax. It is in this sense that the trust is "simple." There are no after-tax accumulations which increase the corpus/capital of the trust.

General Format, Page 1

The head portion of Form 1041 is where most initial mistakes are made. The information entered in the spaces and indicated by the checkboxes is used by the IRS computer for setting up its tracking program on each Tax ID number (EIN) issued to a trust. Once the computer tracking program gets going, you'll have difficulty correcting any errors you may have made.

One of the most frequently made errors — because it **is** a source of initial confusion — is *Date entity created* (Block D in Figure 6.1). This is a specific calendar date which is repeated on Form 1041 year after year, as long as the trust is in operation. A trust is "created" when it becomes irrevocably funded and earns its first $1 or more of tax accountable income. If you mistakenly enter some date prior to the first $1 of earnings, you are computer compelled to file Forms 1041 for all nonearning years.

With the above in mind, we present in Figure 6.2 the general format of page 1 of Form 1041. As you can see, there are three "working portions," namely: *income, deductions,* and *tax payments.* In other words, page 1 is a summary page entirely.

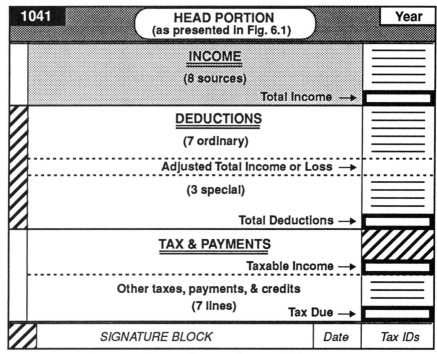

Fig. 6.2 - General Format: Page 1 of Form 1041

As with all summary pages on tax returns, every line on which an entry is made must be backed up with an attachment of some sort. The attachment may be a nonofficial self-explanatory format, or an applicable official schedule or form. Generally, there are between 5 and 15 attachments to most Forms 1041. The number of attachments is not contingent upon whether a simple or complex trust is involved. The number is more related to the diversity of income sources and the types of deductions claimed by the trustee.

For example, in the income portion of page 1, the following attachments are required, where applicable:

Schedule B (1040) — Interest and Dividend Income
Schedule C (1040) — Profit or Loss from Business
Schedule D (1041) — Capital Gains and Losses
Schedule E (1040) — Supplemental Income and Loss
Form 4562   — Depreciation and Amortization
Form 4797   — Sales of Business Property

Note the mixture of schedules indicated by "1040" and "1041." Many of the schedules and forms that attach to Form 1040 also attach to Form 1041.

In the deduction portion of page 1, the following schedules and forms are mentioned:

Form 4952   — Investment Interest Expense Deduction
Schedule A (1041) — Charitable Deduction
Schedule B (1041) — Income Distribution Deduction

Other applicable deductions require supportive nonofficial attachments.

Income Distribution Deduction

There is one unique deduction feature that clearly distinguishes Form 1041 from Form 1040. This is the income distribution deduction. It is set apart by a separate line in the deductions portion of page 1. Said line reads—

Income distribution deduction (from Schedule B)
Attach Schedules K-1 (Form 1041)

There is no corresponding income deduction line anywhere on Form 1040. This trust deduction is truly unique.

The income distribution deduction for a trust is authorized by Section 651 of the IR Code. This section is titled: ***Deduction for Trusts Distributing Current Income Only.*** It reads in part as—

In the case of any trust the terms of which—

> *(1) provide that all of its income is required to be distributed currently, and*
> *(2) do not provide that any amounts are to be paid, permanently set aside, or used for . . . charitable purposes,*

*there **shall be allowed as a deduction in computing taxable income of the trust** the amount . . . which is required to be distributed currently.* [Emphasis added.]

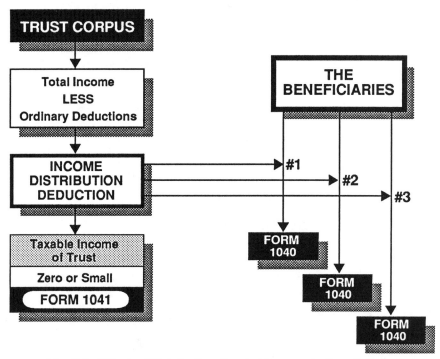

Fig. 6.3 - Effect of Distributing Current Income to Beneficiaries

There is a clear rationale for allowing a "distribution deduction." It sets the stage for determining the amount of the distribution that is taxed to the beneficiaries. This is the gist of Section 652: *Inclusion of Amounts in Gross Income of Beneficiaries of Trusts Distributing Current Income Only*. This is the reason we indicated earlier that a simple trust can actually reduce its tax to zero, or nearly so. If it is not taxed to the trust, it is taxed to the beneficiaries . . . or vice versa. This is one case where, as we depict in Figure 6.3, "tax shifting" is perfectly legitimate.

In a complex trust, the income distribution deduction, while allowed, has to meet more restrictive conditions. Said restrictions are prescribed by Sections 661 and 662 of the IR Code. The deduction involves a complex computation called: *Distributable net income* (DNI). The DNI takes into account amounts paid to, or set aside for, charity; tax-exempt income "allocable" to charity; and any capital gains which are allocable to corpus and paid, or set aside for, charity. The term "set aside" implies accumulations of income and capital gains whereby the charity is viewed as a tax shelter for less needy beneficiaries. Thus, it is the charitable set aside feature that makes a trust complex. Similarly for other set-aside features.

Exemption Amounts Compared

An exemption amount is a form of deduction (though not called so) that is applied before arriving at the taxable income on a return. Whether a 1040 or 1041 return, the sequence for arriving at taxable income is:

Step 1 — Total income	$_____
Step 2 — Adjustments to income	<_____>
Step 3 — Adjusted total income (subtract step 2 from step 1)	_____
Step 4 — Total deductions	<_____>
Step 5 — Taxable income *before* exemption amount (subtract step 4 from step 3)	_____
Step 6 — Exemption amount	<_____>
Step 7 — Taxable income (subtract step 6 from step 5)	$_____

A simple trust is allowed a flat $300 exemption per year; a complex trust is allowed only $100. Unlike individual exemptions, the amounts are not adjusted for cost of living (inflation) year after year. Being nonhuman entities that they are, trusts do not engender high political priority.

Human individuals are allowed much higher exemption amounts than are trusts. A single person in 2002 was allowed a $3,000 exemption. Each year, a cost of living adjustment is applied. By comparison with a trust, a single person enjoys nearly a $3,000 exemption advantage. This feature alone certainly suggests that, when given the option, income distributions to beneficiaries are the better way to go.

Tax Rate Bands Compared

An even stronger incentive for making all possible income distributions to beneficiaries is the differences in the tax rate bands. A "rate band" is the spread in income amounts that is subject to the same tax rate. The federal ordinary income tax rates range from a low of 10% to a maximum of 35% (as of tax year 2004). The rate band — spread in income amount — differs markedly between a trust and an individual (single status).

For comparison purposes, here are the 2004 income bands and their corresponding tax rates (there is no 10% rate for trusts):

Trust	Tax Rate	Single Person
0 – $1,950	15%	7,150 – $ 29,050
1,950 – 4,600	25%	29,050 – 70,350
4,600 – 7,000	28%	70,350 – 146,750
7,000 – 9,550	33%	146,750 – 319,100
over 9,550	35%	over 319,100

This tabulation alone should convince you that it is far better to pass through — distribute — all of the taxable income that you can to the beneficiaries. Trusts simply are not intended to be tax shelters for wealthy beneficiaries, nor are they a means of accumulating great wealth for distributions to generations down the line. The great trust sheltering days of the past are virtually gone.

To put our point in perspective, let us consider that the taxable income (after the appropriate exemption) Step 7 above is $20,000.

If left in the trust, the tax would be about $7,000. If distributed to a single beneficiary, the tax on $20,000 would be $3,000 (assuming no other income from other sources to the beneficiary). From this simple comparison, it is clearly more tax advantageous to distribute income to beneficiaries than not to distribute to them.

There could be situations where it is administratively more practical to retain "odd-dollar" de minimis amounts of taxable income in the trust. For example, suppose there were five beneficiaries, each of whom was "promised" by the trustor that he/she would receive $20,000 per year for life. This would be a required income distribution of $100,000 (5 x $20,000). Suppose it turned out that the amount actually available for distribution were $102,800. From a practical point of view, it would be better to leave the $2,800 in the trust than to try to split such a small amount five ways. Generally speaking, if the retained taxable amount is 5% or less of the total distributable amount, the trust would **not** lose its "simple trust" classification.

What If There's Loss?

Exemptions and tax rates apply only where there is positive net income. What happens if there is *negative* net income? That is, there's a net loss for the operational year? This introduces a new tax term: Net Operating Loss (NOL).

A trust is a legal entity which is tax treated as a business entity of its own. The effect is that when an operating loss occurs for the accounting year, the entity retains the loss unto itself. It is **not** distributed to the beneficiaries as would be the case for positive net income. An exception exists only for the year in which the trust terminates. Otherwise, the loss is carried forward — in the trust — year after year until it is eventually absorbed by positive income generated in downstream years.

With regard to NOLs, instructions to Form 1041 state as follows:

*If line [taxable income] is a loss, the trust may have a net operating loss (NOL). Do **not** include the deductions claimed on lines [charitable deduction, income distribution deduction,* and exemption] *when figuring the amount of the NOL. An NOL generally may be carried . . . forward to the following 15 tax years. Complete Schedule A of Form 1045: Application for Tentative Refund, to figure the amount of NOL that is available for carryover.*

Surely, in 15 eligible carryforward years, any NOL can be absorbed by the trust. If the trust terminates before full absorption, the unused NOL carryforward becomes an allowable distribution to the beneficiaries.

More Checkboxes & Questions

Page 2 of Form 1041 is partitioned into four sections, namely:

- Schedule A (Charitable Deduction),
- Schedule B (Income Distribution Deduction),
- Schedule G (Tax Computation), and
- Other Information.

We'll come back to Schedules A, B, and G in subsequent chapters when more pertinent.

The entire lower portion of page 2 consists of a series of eight questions and checkboxes labeled: *Other Information.* These questions and checkboxes have an important bearing on how the IRS processes your trust return. In highly abbreviated form, we present the eight questions to you in Figure 6.4. We've abbreviated them primarily for space reasons, but also because you can grasp their significance better.

For example, Question 1 in Figure 6.4 simply asks—

Any tax-exempt income? ☐ *Yes* ☐ *No*
*If "Yes," enter amount $*_____

Compare this abbreviation with the same question 1 on an official Form 1041. The question reads in full as—

FORM 1041	OTHER INFORMATION	Page 2 Lower		
			Yes	No
1.	Any tax-exempt income? _____ - if "yes", enter amount. $_____			
2.	Any assignment of personal earnings (salary, wages, compensation) by contract?			
3.	Any foreign financial accounts?_____ - if "yes", enter country. _____			
4.	Any transfer to a foreign trust? _____ - if "yes", file proper forms (3520, etc.).			
5.	Any seller financed mortgage interest? _____ - if "yes", enter name & tax IDs.			
6.	Check if Sec. 643 (e)(3) election. (noncash distributions)	▶ ☐		
7.	Check if Sec. 663 (b) election. (65-day grace period)	▶ ☐		
8.	Check if estate open more than 2 years.	▶ ☐		

Fig. 6.4 - The Special "Must Answer" Checkboxes on Form 1041

Did the trust receive any tax-exempt income? If "Yes," attach a computation of the allocation of expenses. Enter the amount of tax-exempt interest income and exempt-interest dividends.

The 1041 instructions regarding Question 1 say—

If the trust received tax-exempt income, figure the allocation of expenses between tax-exempt and taxable income on a separate sheet and attach it to the return. . . . Expenses that are directly [or indirectly] allocable to tax-exempt income are allocated only to tax-exempt income. . . . No deduction that would otherwise be allowable for taxable income is allowed for any expense that is allocable to tax-exempt income. . . . Enter only the deductible amounts [against taxable income] on the return.

This instruction is the fallout from longstanding tradition in the taxation world. Any expenses — any whatsoever — attributable to the generation of tax-exempt income are **not allowed** as a deduction on a return (period!). Consequently, if you answer "Yes" to Question 1, you **must attach** a statement showing what the allocable expenses were. If truly no allocable expenses were incurred, make a convincing statement to this effect. Otherwise, guess what will happen?

The IRS's computer will *add* the tax-exempt income to the total income reported on the return. This will give an "aggregate income": tax-exempt plus taxable. The ratio of exempt income to aggregate income becomes the **disallowance ratio** which is then applied to *all* deductions on the return. Such is the "power" of tax form checkboxes and the IRS's computer. No IRS human ever checks on the disallowance mechanics.

Any Wages Assigned?

Question 2 in Figure 6.4 is another computer tax trap. A "Yes" on Question 2 means that the 1041 you file as a simple trust will be returned with instructions to refile it as a grantor type trust. Let us explain.

Question 2 reads officially as—

*Did the trust receive all or any part of the earnings (salary, wages, and other compensation) **of any individual** by reason of a contract assignment or similar arrangement?* ☐ *Yes* ☐ *No*

Before this question is answered too casually, you'd better first read the instructions. They say—

*All salaries, wages, and other compensation **for personal services** must be included on the return of the person who earned the income, even if the income was irrevocably assigned to the trust by a contract assignment or similar arrangement.*

The grantor or person creating the [assignment] *is considered the owner* [of the trust] *if he or she keeps "beneficial enjoyment" of, or substantial control over, the trust property . . .* [such as when] *the trust pays the living expenses for the grantor and the grantor's family.*

If you checked "Yes" to Question 2, [refile as] ***Grantor Type Trust.***

The grantor trust rules require that all income, deductions, and credits allocable to the grantor be reported on Form 1040: **not** on Form 1041. One cannot use a trust to "shelter" his/her personal service earnings and thereby avoid income tax, social security tax, and medicare tax on those earnings. The only income reportable on Form 1041 is that which is generated exclusively by the trust property itself. Even then, the property must be irrevocably assigned after all transfer taxes (gift/death/GST) have been paid. Those trust promoters who have led you to believe otherwise, have done you a disservice.

Foreign Accounts & Trusts

Questions 3 and 4 in Figure 6.4 address those foreign accounts and foreign trusts which have any relationship to the trust of which you are the trustee. There is nothing improper or illegal about having foreign entity associations with your trust. It just means that you have a lot of other tax forms to prepare and file. Such filings are separate and apart from Form 1041.

Question 3 in the "Other Information" portion of page 2 on Form 1041 reads—

*At any time during the calendar year, did the trust have an interest in or a signature or other authority over a bank, securities, or other financial account in a foreign country? See instructions for exceptions and filing requirements for **Form TD F 90-22.1**. If "Yes," enter the name of the foreign country* [or countries].

The pertinent instructions say—

* *Check "No" . . . if the combined value of all accounts of the trust was $10,000 or less during the whole year . . .* [in one or more foreign accounts].

- *Check "Yes" . . . if the trust owns more than 50% of the stock in any corporation that owns one or more foreign bank accounts.*

- *If you checked "Yes" to Question 3, file Form TD F 90-22.1:* **Report of Foreign Bank and Financial Accounts** *with the Department of the Treasury at the address shown on the form. Do not file with Form 1041.*

Question 4 opens up a Pandora's box of still additional forms to file. This question officially reads:

During the tax year, did the trust receive a distribution from, or was it a grantor of or transferor to, a foreign trust? If "Yes," see the instructions for other forms the trust may have to file.

These "other forms" are—

Form 926 — Return by a U.S. Transferor of Property to a Foreign Corporation, Foreign Estate or Trust, or Foreign Partnership.

Form 3520 — Creation of or Transfers to Certain Foreign Trusts.

Form 3520A — Annual Return of Foreign Trust with U.S. Beneficiaries.

As you may sense from the above, things can get complicated. Questions 5, 6, 7, and 8 in Figure 6.4 add still more complications, if the options apply. This brings us to our summary point of this chapter. If, as trustee, you go much beyond distributing current income (and some corpus perhaps) to the beneficiaries, you take on complications which probably were not intended by the original (gratuitous) trustor(s).

7

SOURCES OF TRUST INCOME

Property Assigned To The Trust Is Preferably Of A Type Which Produces Current Income. There Are Eight Potential Sources Of Such Income Which Are Taxable. Four Are Almost Always Positive And Four May Be Either Positive Or Negative (Meaning: LOSS). Loss Sources Are Inadvisable. Even So, Schedule D (1041): Capital Gains And Losses, Should Be Retained For Converting From One Trust Investment To Another. The Most Desired Form Of Trust Property Is Rental Real Estate. There Are Also Three NONTAXABLE Sources Of Income. They Tend To Be Ignored In The Official Instructions Accompanying Form 1041.

Take out your latest personal Form 1040 return, and count the number of income source lines preprinted on it. Altogether, there are 14 such lines. Of this number, five are group-classed as *personal service income.* They are:

- Wages, salaries, tips, etc.
- Alimony received
- Pensions and annuities
- Unemployment compensation
- Social security benefits

Now, take out a trust Form 1041 and glance at the preprinted income lines thereon. There are no corresponding personal service income lines, are there? The reason is obvious (or should be).

A trust is a nonhuman (though legal) entity. As such it cannot generate personal service income on its own. It does not need to, because there are so many other sources of income which the trust *property* can generate. Thus, the key distinction between a valid trust and an invalid one is the absence of personal service income.

Those trust arrangements which accept any assignment of personal service earnings by the trustor, trustee, beneficiary, or other person are classed as grantor-type trusts. They do not file Form 1041; they file Form 1040. Personal service earnings are subject to social security and medicare tax, whereas valid trusts are not.

Consequently, in this chapter we want to cover the legitimate sources of income that a valid trust may have. By describing the sources briefly, you will get a better idea of how to arrange the trust property for maximum income. If all or most of the income is distributed to the beneficiaries, the trust pays little or no tax.

There Are 8 Sources

In Figure 6.2 we presented a blank layout of Form 1041. In the income portion we indicated "8 sources." Now, we enumerate these sources exactly as preprinted on page 1 of Form 1041—

1. *Interest income*
2. *Dividends*
3. *Business income or (loss)*
4. *Capital gain or (loss)*
5. *Rents, royalties, partnerships, other estates and trusts, etc.*
6. *Farm income or (loss)*
7. *Ordinary gain or (loss)*
8. *Other income. List type and amount.*

Interest and dividend income is that which is derived from (commercially available) investment sources. Business and farm income/loss are classed as "trade or business" income. Capital gain/ loss and ordinary gain/loss are classed as "transactional" income. It is important to note that trade or business and transactional income recognize *losses*. In contrast, there are no losses recognized under interest and dividend income sources.

Some persons are very sensitive to losses. They construe every tax-recognized loss as deliberate fraud and misrepresentation. They are ready to sue at the drop of a pin. This means that if you have some loss-sensitive beneficiaries, or you are being hawk-eyed by some covetous professional, you probably should tread lightly with trade or business and transactional activities. The problem could be that if you are too conservative and invest only in interest and dividend sources, you could be criticized for that too. Trying to steer a middle prudent course is not always easy to do.

All trustees have to face what we call "the middle course dilemma." This is the very reason why income-producing real estate is the favored form of trust property investment. Real estate can produce rents and royalties (from natural resource extraction) which, more often than not, net out as positive income. Beneficiaries and watchdogs like this.

Interest & Dividend Income

The simplest and safest form of income to a trust is through interest and dividends. Once the income sources have been selected, and trust money is allocated to them, it is a matter of sitting back and collecting the payments. As they come in, you post them into the checking-only working account which we suggested back in Figure 5.1. Identify each item of your deposited income for end-of-year reconciliations.

When setting up each interest- and dividend-paying account, make sure that the payer has the trust's correct Tax ID number. Each account also should be identified with the trust's correct name. The trust — not the trustee — is the recipient and accountable entity for the income. At the end of the year, the payer will provide you with what is called "1099 information" on each account that has been established. The payer does this with the following forms (or their substitutes):

Form 1099-INT: *Interest Income*
Form 1099-OID: *Original Issue Discount*
Form 1099-DIV: *Dividends and Distributions*

These are information returns which are sent electronically by the payers to the IRS. All three of these reporting-to-IRS forms contain a box labeled: *Federal income tax withheld.* Our strong urging is that you NOT permit the payer to withhold any federal tax from the trust income. Chances are, the trust would have little or no tax to pay. Yet, if you inadvertently allow withholding to take place, you have to claim a refund of it when the trust's 1041 return is filed. This clutters up your trust accounting unnecessarily.

There is one 1099 form that is guaranteed to give you nightmares. It is Form 1099-OID: Original Issue Discount. There is an asterisked footnote on the form which reads:

> *The* [box 1 amount] *may not be the correct figure to report on your tax return. See instruction* [hereto].

The instructions go on to say that—

> *OID is the difference between the stated redemption price at maturity and the issue price of a bond, debenture, note, or other evidence of indebtedness, or the acquisition price of a stripped bond or coupon, or other deposit arrangement where the payment of interest is deferred until maturity. . . . OID is taxable over the life of the obligation. You must include a part of the OID in your gross income each year you hold the obligation.*

Form 1099-DIV contains five boxes of dollar amounts which you should extract carefully and enter on the trust's 1041 return. These boxes are alphabetized as follows:

1(a) — *Total ordinary dividends*
1(b) — *Qualified dividends*
2(a) — *Capital gain distributions*
3(a) — *Nontaxable distributions*
5(a) — *Investment expenses*

Where you can, it is always desirable to put trust money into corporate stocks which pay both ordinary dividends **and** capital gains. The higher these payments are, the better.

Use Schedule B: Form 1040

When dealing with trust money and trust property, you (as trustee) want to have as many attachments as possible to the trust's Form 1041. Attachments to an official tax return convey authenticity and "no playing around with the numbers." Even the most skeptical beneficiary or most covetous attorney will "back off" when you can produce an official tax document filed with the IRS.

In the case of interest and dividend income, there is no required attachment to Form 1041. Its page 1 line entries simply read—

1. *Interest income* $_____
2. *Dividends* $_____

Even though not required, our suggestion is that you prepare and attach **Schedule B (Form 1040):** *Interest and Dividend Income*, to Form 1041. Be aware that this is a 1040 schedule: not a 1041. The information required is identical.

For each interest-bearing account and, **separately**, for each dividend-paying account, use a separate entry line on the Schedule B (1040). For each account, enter the gross amount received followed by any authorized adjustments. By making each entry for each account self-explanatory, you are presenting a prima facie case of trying to do things right.

When reporting dividends, there are preprinted provisions for adjustments for (a) capital gain distributions and (b) nontaxable distributions. For example, if the trust received $1,000 gross dividends from the PDQ Mutual Fund (including $350 in capital gains and $150 in nontaxables), you would enter as follows:

PDQ Fund		$1,000
Capital gains	350	
Nontaxables	150	
		<500>
	Net dividends	$ 500

Technically, all you have to do is enter $500 on line 2 (dividends) on Form 1041. No Schedule B (1040) is required. But if some watchdog over you learned that the trust received $1,000 in dividends, and you only reported $500, can't you sense the suspicions that would be aroused? With Schedule B (1040) filled in correctly, you've done the proper accounting well ahead of time.

Directly Owned Real Estate

Many trustors build their retirement and afterlife wealth through rental real estate. They do so because rental properties possess three choice ingredients, namely:

(1) Potential for appreciation over long periods of time,
(2) Income production through rents, royalties, and similar user fees,
(3) Tax sheltering through mortgage interest deductions and depreciation allowances for buildings, structures, and improvements.

The preferred property includes residential buildings, commercial structures, natural resource deposits, and sharecropping farmland.

Unlike stocks, bonds, mutual funds, and mortgage notes, real estate is illiquid. Though marketable over time, it is not readily disposable at will. This means that a trustor who owned real estate during life will most likely have assigned his holdings to a trust. This is great, providing the real estate in trust produces a net positive income of 6 percent or more. Recall our discussion in Chapter 5 on rearranging trust property.

During life, most real estate owners mortgage their property to the hilt and maximize their depreciation allowance, so that the net income is negative (meaning loss). This provides tax sheltering to other positive income sources, such as wages and salaries. With property in trust, however, the tax sheltering motivation is diminished. More preferably, net *positive* income is sought. This means paying down, as much as is prudent, any existing mortgages. Subsequently, the positive income is passed through to the beneficiaries who pay tax at diluted rates.

Income produced from rental real estate is reported on Form 1041 via Schedule E (Form 1040), Part I. On this point, the preprinted instructions on the rents and royalties income line of Form 1041 say—

5. *Rents, royalties, . . . etc. Attach Schedule E (Form 1040).*

A digest of this schedule is presented in Figure 7.1. We have omitted the portions of the official schedule which address the at-risk and passive loss limitation rules. With net positive income from trust property, you can ignore these special rules.

Sch. E (1040)	INCOME OR LOSS FROM RENTAL REAL ESTATE AND ROYALTIES					Part I
Property Kind and Location				Continuation Schedules		
A B C			[1]	[2]	[3]	
INCOME	A	B	C	D,E,F	G,H,I	TOTALS
Rents						
Royalties						
EXPENSES						
14 Items						
Depreciation						
Depletion						
TOTAL EXPENSES						
Income						
Loss						
				NET INCOME OR LOSS ➡		

Fig. 7.1 - Accommodation of Multiple Properties on Schedule E (1040), Part 1

Although Schedule E (1040), Part I, is formatted for three rental properties (A, B, C), it is not uncommon for some trusts to own 5, 10, or more such properties. In this case, you use multiple forms. You sequentially number the forms, and re-alphabetize the preprinted vertical columns as D, E, F; G, H, I; J, K, L . . . etc. For each parcel of rental/royalty property, there must be a separate columnar display of income, expenses, and depreciation (or depletion in the case of natural resource property). When each property is fully accounted for, care is required to extend all entries through to ONE total column at the far right. We try to portray this one total column for you in Figure 7.1.

If the trust owns farm property which is being rented or share-cropped, an entirely different form is required. This is **Form 4835**: *Farm Rental Income and Expenses*. Its arrangement is similar to that of Schedule E, Part I. However, it has additional preprinted income and expense lines which are peculiar to farming operations and subsidy payments.

Indirectly Owned Real Estate, Etc.

Real estate is capital intensive. This generally means that a single trust doesn't have the financial resources to engage in large projects such as apartment buildings, shopping malls, superstores, prestigious hotels, yacht harbors, off-shore mining, and the like. Participation in these projects requires that the trust pool some of its money with that of other investors (of all types).

Pooled investments are more beneficial through pass-through entities such as partnerships, S corporations, other trusts, and real estate mortgage investment conduits (REMICs). While a trustee exercises no direct supervision of these entities, one must always be leery of the marketing hype often associated with pooled-investment projects. Seek only those which are *income* oriented rather than tax shelter oriented.

One of the advantages of pass-through entity investment projects is that, in addition to income distributions, there are also distributions of certain deductions, credits, and capital gains (and losses). These and other pass-through features derive from the fact that partnerships, S corporations, other trusts, and REMICs are not taxable entities. This is unlike investing in large C corporations where, primarily, dividends only are paid.

Distributions from pass-through entities are reported to the IRS — then to you as trustee — on the following official forms (or their substitutes):

Partnership: *Schedule K-1 (1065)* — Partner's Share of Income, Credits, Deductions, etc.

S corporation: *Schedule K-1 (1120S)* — Shareholder's Share of Income, Credits, Deductions, etc.

Other Trust: *Schedule K-1 (1041)* — Beneficiary's Share of Income, Deductions, Credits, etc.

REMIC: *Schedule Q (1066)* — Notice to Residual Interest Holder of Taxable Income or Net Loss Allocation

All of these information returns are pulled together and entity identified on Schedule E (1040), Parts II, III, and IV. This is the same Schedule E (1040) that you attach to the trust's Form 1041 when directly owning rental and royalty property. The only difference is that the trust's directly owned property is identified in Part I, whereas the indirectly owned property is identified in Parts II, III, and IV. We schematize the reporting arrangement for you in Figure 7.2. Notice the entry in Part V: Net Farm Rentals.

Then, at the bottom of Schedule E (its Part V), all income is summarized and entered as one figure on page 1 of Form 1041. Entry is made at the line designated as—

Rents, royalties, partnerships, other trusts, etc.
Attach Schedule E (Form 1040)

Transactional Gains & Losses

A "transaction" is the sale or exchange of property — trust property in our case. The property may be corporate stock, mutual fund shares, long-term bonds, residential real estate, commercial real estate, farm land, natural resource land, machinery and equipment, collectibles (works of art, coins, guns, stamps, antiques, etc.) . . . and anything else whose unit value varies over time. It is because of value variations over time that a transactional event produces either gain, no gain/no loss, or loss.

Sch. E (1040)	SUPPLEMENTAL INCOME AND LOSS		Page 2
Part II	Partnerships & S Corporations		Special Rules
/////	Description of Entity	INCOME	LOSS
A			
B			
C			
D			
E			
Part III	Estates & Trusts	//////	//////
A			
B			
Part IV	Real Estate Mortgage Conduits	//////	//////
A			
B			
Part V	Summary (Including Part I)	//////	//////
Form 4835: Net Farm Rentals			
Transfer: Net from Part I			
//////////	Totals		< >
//////////	NET INCOME OR LOSS ➤		

Fig. 7.2 - Other Forms of Property Holdings on Schedule E (1040), Page 2

For trust tax accounting, there are two distinct categories of transactional events. The first category is **Schedule D**: *Capital Gains and Losses;* the second category is **Form 4797**: *Ordinary Gains and Losses*. What's the difference?

The difference is that Form 4797 events involve business-use property where *depreciation or depletion* has been claimed as a deduction allowance over the years of productive ownership. These allowances apply to rental real estate, natural resource deposits, trucks and tractors, breeder animals, fruit trees and vines, etc.

If, during the year, an item of business property is sold, the procedure is to prepare Form 4797 first, then Schedule D. The reason for this is that with business property there is potential for *recapture gain* (Part III of Form 4797). This is a combination of ordinary gain and capital gain. The capital gain portion transfers to Schedule D, whereas the ordinary gain portion stays on Form 4797. Furthermore, if business property held more than one year results in a capital loss, it converts to an ordinary loss and stays on Form 4797. The ordinary losses on Form 4797 are not subject to any statutory limitation. The overall result is that Form 4797 is more complicated than Schedule D.

Schedule D, however, has some special rules of its own. Net capital gain (short-term or long-term) can be passed through to the beneficiaries, allocably. Net capital loss (short-term or long-term) remains in the trust where it is carried forward from year to year. Only $3,000 of the net loss can be used in a given year. For these reasons, a specially designed Schedule D (1041) for trusts is used.

A schematic representation of the relationship between Schedule D (1041), Form 4797, and Form 1041 is presented in Figure 7.3. As depicted in the figure, when all transactional gain/loss reportings are complete, their totals transfer to the income portion of Form 1041 at the following lines:

    4. *Capital gain or (loss). Attach Schedule D (1041).*
    7. *Ordinary gain or (loss). Attach Form 4797.*

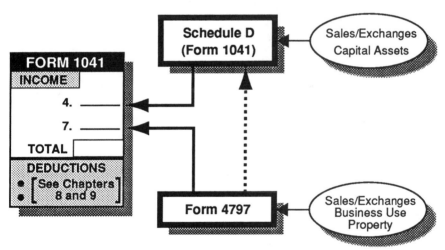

Fig. 7.3 - Attachments to Form 1041 When Making Sales or Exchanges

Business & Farm Income

For trust purposes, income generated from a trade or business, or from a farming operation, is that which is held in sole proprietorship form. The operation is continuous and ongoing on a regular basis. It may be a retail store, a manufacturing shop, a sales organization, a repair and maintenance service, a farm or ranch or orchard or vineyard, a fishing company, or other proprietorship activity. The activity may generate net income, or it may generate a net loss. Either way, it is classed as a "material participation" activity because of the long, hard hours required to keep such activities alive.

Generally, a proprietorship business or farm is trust-inherited from the trustor(s). As such, the trust continues the activity long enough until either the profits run out or it can be sold. Continuing an unprofitable business or farm is inadvisable in a trust. Unlike a partnership or S corporation, the trust does not need the tax sheltering benefits of a loss activity. Consequently, it is also inadvisable to launch into a new business or new farming operation with liquid assets acquired from other sources of trust income.

Where there is a proprietorship business or farm owned by the trust, it is not expected that you, as trustee, run the operation day by day. You're expected to hire managers and employees to do the routine work. Otherwise, day-to-day oversight and management is distractive and time consuming. It can sap much time and energy from your other trustee duties.

There is truly one unique tax feature that arises when a trust owns a proprietorship business or farm. It is: no self-employment tax applies. The self-employment tax is a combination of social security and medicare tax; it is computed on Schedule SE. The SE tax applies to all filers of **Schedule C (1040)**: *Profit or Loss from Business*, or **Schedule F (1040)**: *Profit or Loss from Farming*. It is a surtax for the privilege of making a profit in a material participation activity. If there is a net loss on Schedules C or F, the SE tax does not apply.

At the **Net profit or (loss)** line on Schedules C or F, there is a small-print instruction which reads:

[For Schedule C filers]: *Trusts, enter on Form 1041, line 3.*

[For Schedule F filers]: *Trusts, enter on Form 1041, line 6.*

These profit instructions for trusts bypass Schedule SE altogether.

If there is a net loss either on Schedule C or Schedule F, another instruction says—

If you have a loss, check the box that describes your investment in this activity:

☐ *All investment is at risk.*
☐ *Some investment is not at risk.*

Regardless of which investment-risk box you check, beneficiaries are not going to be very happy if you (as trustee) incur business or farm losses year after year.

Three "Heavy Hitters"

For purposes of a trust, loss sources of income are not desired. They benefit no one. A trust is **not** a tax shelter. The 1041 losses do not pass through to the beneficiaries for offsetting other positive sources of 1040 income.

If you will glance at the 8 sources of 1041 income listed back on page 7-2, you'll note that there are four potential loss types. These loss potentials are source 3: Business income or loss; source 4: Capital gain or loss; source 6: Farm income or loss; and source 7: Ordinary gain or loss. Our surmise is that after the first few years of trust operation, at least three of the four loss sources would likely be eliminated . . . or at least significantly curtailed.

Accordingly, we believe that once a trust operation settles down into its long-term mode, the only loss potential would be income source 4: Capital gain or loss. This will always be an ongoing source. This is because it is the transactional "facilitator" for changing from one investment vehicle to another, as new opportunities for growth and income present themselves. Furthermore, source 4 enables the trustee to liquefy assets at any time, should prudence suggest that he do so.

Over time, the "heavy hitters" in a trust portfolio are likely to be source 1 (interest), source 2 (dividends), and source 5 (rents, etc.). Whether by design or inertia, most family created trusts tend to evolve into such a pattern. The evolution is a matter — simply — of conservative management of trust property. A trust, after all, is not expected to continue indefinitely. Its mission is to exist only so long as necessary to distribute income and corpus equitably to all designated beneficiaries.

Nontaxable Income

Another aspect of conservative trust management is to generate as much nontaxable income as is legitimately possible. On this point, official instructions on how to treat and record such income are totally silent. It is as though the IRS hopes that you, as trustee, will become bewildered and inadvertently list all nontaxable income as source 8 on Form 1041: "Other income." **Do not let this happen to you!**

Although nontaxable income is not tax accountable it **is** fully trust accountable. This means that you have to keep a parallel set of records with those for taxable income, as illustrated by Figure 7.4. Do not try to hide the nontaxable income. Keep an accurate running record so that you could lay it out on the table, should the IRS become suspicious and make demands on you. Engaging in foreign trusts and off-shore tax havens is probably one of the worst things you can do as a trustee.

What are the kinds of nontaxable income that come within the purview of your trustee duties? There are three, namely:

(1)   Return-of-capital income,
(2)   Tax-benefit income, and
(3)   Tax-exempt income.

Return-of-capital income is where source 4: Schedule D, stands out. The column (e) on Schedule D (Capital Gains and Losses) reads—

Cost or other basis. See instructions.

A trust's tax basis in a transactional event is its "return of capital." Any return of capital is not taxed. This is because it has been

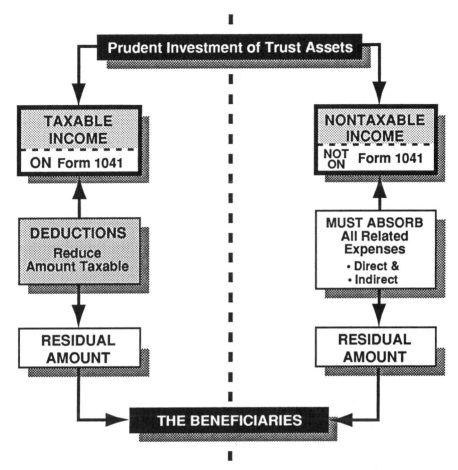

Fig. 7.4 - The Comparative Roles of Taxable and Nontaxable Income

previously taxed, either through prior income taxation or transfer taxation. The instructions to column (e) mention other items that can increase the return of capital.

Tax- benefit income comprises those "tax savings" derived from allowances for amortization, depletion, depreciation, and casualty deductions. Consider, for example, that the trust owns some residential rental property. Suppose the depreciation allowance amounted to $5,000 per year. The net effect is that $5,000 of otherwise taxable rental income becomes nontaxable. There is nothing devious about this. It is a direct fallout from the proper use of tax rules.

Tax-exempt income is expressly nontaxable in the Internal Revenue Code. We refer you to Section 108: *Interest on State and Local Bonds.* Its subsection (a) reads—

Exclusion. Except as provided in subsection (b), gross income does not include interest on any State or local bond.

The reference to subsection 108(b) is—

Subsection (a) shall not apply to [any]

(1) Private activity bond which is not a qualified bond,
(2) Arbitrage bond, [or]
(3) Bond not in registered form.

Obviously, our conclusion to this chapter is that the more nontaxable income you generate for the trust, the better. Like taxable income, the nontaxable income is passed through to the beneficiaries. When so passed through, they pay no tax on that income.

As with all good things, however, reality eventually sets in. If all of the trust's income were nontaxable, there would be nothing from which to deduct the various expenses of trust management. Operational expenses and other deductions can only be applied against taxable income.

8

ADMINISTRATIVE DEDUCTIONS

An Operating Trust Is A "Bundle" Of Activities And Properties, Some Of Which Are Income Producing And Some Not. Either Way, Certain Administrative Expenditures Are Required To Keep The Trust On Course. Such Expenses Are Deductible Against Tax-Accountable Income. The Foremost Deductions Are Trustee Fees, Attorney And Accountant Fees, Tax Return Preparation Fees, And — Where Required — Charitable Contributions. Miscellaneous Itemized Deductions (Auto, Travel, Office Supplies, Phone, Fax, Etc.) Are Subject To A 2% AGI "Floor." Losses Are Not Subject To This Floor.

All income tax returns — trust or nontrust — require, first, that all taxable sources of income be totaled. Once these sources are identified and tabulated, another preparatory phase sets in. Said phase is the identification (and justification) of those expenditures which are allowed as *deductions* against the total income. For Form 1041, there are two classes of these deductions. One we call "administrative" deductions; the other we call "distributive" deductions. We'll concentrate in this chapter on the administrative deductions only.

By administrative deductions, we mean those expenditures which the head office of any business would incur when seeking a profit. For a family trust, however, we have to make a distinction between those deductions allowable against the total income of the trust, and those which appear on other attachments to Form 1041.

Attachments such as Schedules C, D, E, F, and Form 4797, all permit deductions for those expenses directly associated with the income reported on those attachments. Obviously, claiming the same deduction twice is prohibited.

Therefore, the focus in this chapter is strictly on those deductible expenses which are incurred for administering the trust overall, rather than on any particular income source of the trust. This category includes interest paid on borrowed money, property and other taxes paid in connection with nonincome-producing assets, fiduciary fees, legal and professional fees, charitable contributions, and other deductions such as auto and travel, office expenses, phone and utilities, office equipment, and so on.

The term "administrative deduction" **does NOT include** the identical (or near-identical) expenses incurred for acquiring and administering sources of tax-exempt income. You must separate out these expenses before totaling the allowable deductions as subtractions against taxable income. Later in this chapter, we'll explain the procedures for making this separation.

When all allowable deductions are totaled, they are subtracted from the total (taxable) income. The result is termed: *Adjusted total income or loss*. If the adjusted total is a loss, it is retained in the trust and not passed through to the beneficiaries.

Overview of Deductions

There is a total of seven types of administrative deductions allowed against the total (taxable) income of the trust. The seven are preprinted on page 1 of Form 1041, starting immediately following the line labeled: *Total income*. The deductions are listed in a separate portion of the 1041 bold-designated as: **Deductions**.

As preprinted and listed on Form 1041, the seven deductions (in official order) are—

1. Interest
2. Taxes
3. Fiduciary fees
4. Charitable deduction
5. Attorney, accountant, and return preparer fees

6. Other deductions NOT subject to 2% floor
7. Miscellaneous deductions SUBJECT to 2% floor

Of the above deductions, the most frustrating are items 6 and 7. Both make reference to a "2% floor." The 2% floor is one of those gimmicky laws that Congress passed in 1986 at the insistence of the IRS. The objective is to curtail the use of miscellaneous deductions that would otherwise reduce tax revenue to government. The specific law on point is Section 67: *2-Percent Floor on Miscellaneous Itemized Deductions*. Its subsection (a) is the general rule, which reads—

In the case of an individual, the miscellaneous itemized deductions for any taxable year shall be allowed only to the extent that the aggregate of such deductions exceeds 2 percent of adjusted gross income.

Note that this general rule addresses only individuals. These are persons who are filers of Form 1040. Other subsections of Section 67 address other classes of filers. Subsection (e), for example, addresses estates and trusts. The Section 67(e) title is: *Determination of Adjusted Gross Income in Case of Estates and Trusts*. Trying to interpret this subsection for Form 1041 purposes is where all the frustration comes.

To give you a little roadmap of where we are heading, we present Figure 8.1. Note that the intermediate line thereon is labeled: *Adjusted total income*. If this line becomes zero or negative (meaning a loss), ordinarily no distributive income deductions can be made to the beneficiaries of the trust.

Interest Paid on Trust Debt

One of the simplest deductions to understand is interest paid on trust debt. If it is investment or business type interest which has not been deducted elsewhere on the 1041 (such as on Schedules C, E, and F), it is a deduction here. This means that the trust has borrowed money to conduct some of its activities. We caution you,

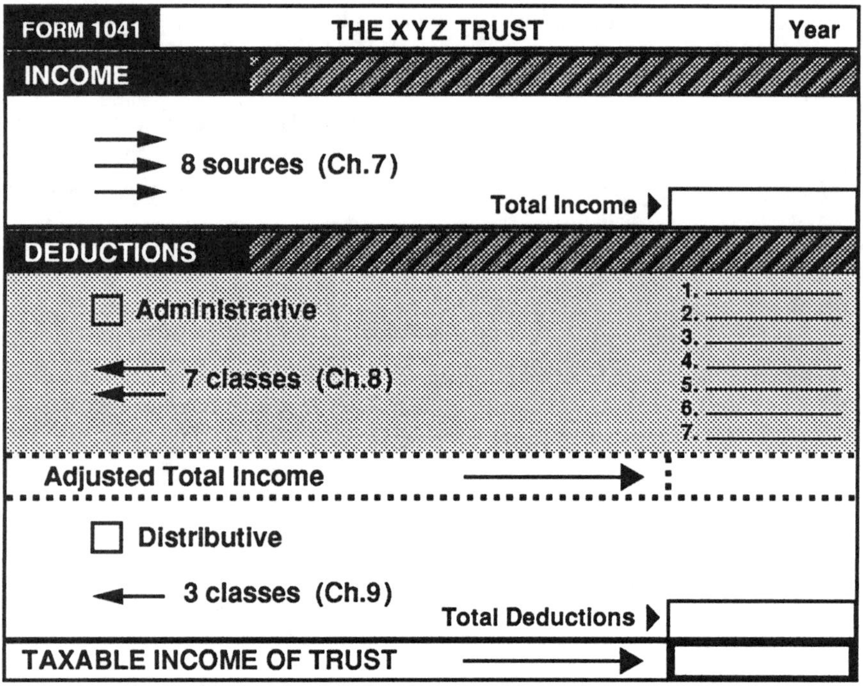

FORM 1041	THE X Y Z TRUST	Year

INCOME

→
→ 8 sources (Ch.7)
→
Total Income ▶

DEDUCTIONS

☐ Administrative

◄ 7 classes (Ch.8)

1. ___
2. ___
3. ___
4. ___
5. ___
6. ___
7. ___

Adjusted Total Income ─────────▶

☐ Distributive

◄ 3 classes (Ch.9)

Total Deductions ▶

TAXABLE INCOME OF TRUST ─────────▶

Fig. 8.1 - Deductions Role of Trust Administration Expenses

though, that too much and too frequent borrowing can jeopardize the perception of you as a prudent trustee.

The official instructions emphasize that there are only three types of interest payments that are deductible. These are—

1. *Any investment interest (subject to limitations);*
2. *Any qualified residence interest; and*
3. *Any interest payable . . . on any unpaid portion of the estate tax attributable to the value of a reversionary or remainder interest in property, or an interest in a closely-held business for the period during which an extension of time for payment of such tax is in effect.*

The term "investment interest" pertains to money borrowed for the acquisition of marketable securities and capital assets, which produce no income while being held. The amount of investment interest deductible in a given year is limited by the amount of taxable investment income (interest, dividends, capital gains) derived during the same year. If the combined amount of investment income is less than the combined amount of investment interest paid out, **Form 4952** must be attached to the 1041. This form is titled: *Investment Interest Expense Deduction.* It provides computationally for carrying forward the unused investment interest to subsequent years.

The 1041 instructions state very clearly—

*Do **not** include interest paid on indebtedness incurred or continued to purchase or carry obligations on which the interest is wholly exempt from income tax.*

This concept is fundamental to all deduction expenditures. You cannot get a deduction for expenses incurred in generating tax-exempt income.

The term "qualified residence interest" pertains to the primary residence of a beneficiary of the trust, who, under the provisions of the trust agreement, is allowed to reside in the residence until his or her death. Honoring this provision is part of the administrative duties of the trustee. Since the trust owns the residence, and the residence generates no income, any mortgage interest paid on the residence is tax deductible.

No other personal-type interest payments by the trust are deductible. The official instructions specifically say—

Personal interest is not deductible. Examples of personal interest include interest paid on:

- *Revolving charge accounts.*
- *Personal notes for money borrowed.*
- *Installment notes on personal use property.*
- *Underpayments of Federal, state, or local income taxes.*

Deductible Taxes Limited

The deduction for taxes paid by the trust is quite limited. It is limited to—

1. Real estate taxes,
2. State and local income taxes, and
3. The generation-skipping transfer tax imposed on income distributions from the trust.

The most common of these three deductibles is real estate taxes. These are property taxes paid or incurred during the year that are not deductible elsewhere on Form 1041. For example, property taxes paid on bare land, on a qualified residence or on other nonincome producing realty would be deductible. Such items as license and registration fees paid on vehicles owned by the trust would not be deductible unless used in a trade or business, or used on a farm.

State and local *sales* taxes are not deductible. Instead, you should treat these taxes as part of the cost of tangible property items. If the items were used in a trade or business, or on a farm, the sales tax would be recovered as part of any depreciation allowance, or as return of capital when the property is sold.

Other taxes that are not deductible are:

(a) Federal income tax,
(b) Federal duties and excise taxes, and
(c) Estate, inheritance, legacy, succession, and gift taxes.

Although state and local *income* taxes are deductible for trusts, said amounts are generally negligible for simple trusts. This is because the taxes are paid primarily by the beneficiaries. In complex trusts, the situation is different because the trust accumulates income which is taxable to it.

As to the generation-skipping transfer tax, our guess is that the deduction would apply to less than 10% of all trusts in operation. Generation-skipping transfers are attractive for trusts whose assets exceed $3,000,000 (3 million).

Fiduciary Fees

A "fiduciary" is *you*, the trustee. It may also be some other responsible person assigned by the probate court to administer the trust estate, should you be unable to serve, or should you be under challenge for your performance of duties.

The instructions to Form 1041 put it this way:

A fiduciary is a trustee of a trust . . . or other person in possession of property of a decedent's estate. A fiduciary takes title to property for the purpose of protecting or conserving it for the beneficiaries. The fiduciary (or one of the joint fiduciaries) must file Form 1041 for a domestic trust taxable under Section 641 [Imposition of Tax on Estates and Trusts].

Normally, fiduciaries are paid compensation for their services rendered on behalf of the trust. We addressed this subject back in Chapter 3: Legal Duties of Trustees. Thus, you are entitled to reasonable compensation for performing your trust duties. The amount of compensation authorized for you **is deductible** as a recognized administrative expense of the trust. This compensation, however, is not tax-free to you.

As the fiduciary and trustee, you must prepare and file Form 1041, with all of its required attachments. In addition, you must also prepare and file **Form 1099-MISC**. This form lists the trust's Tax ID as the payer, and your name and social security number as the recipient/payee. This "information return" is required whenever the trust pays you $600 or more in a given year. The amount paid to you is entered in the box labeled: *Nonemployee compensation.* You are not an employee of the trust. As such, you are not subject to employer withholdings. However, on your own personal Form 1040, you are subject to income tax **and** self-employment tax on your nonemployee compensation.

Charitable Contributions

In the case of a trust contributing to qualified charities, the IRS does lose tax revenue. This is because such charities are classed as *exempt organizations.* That is, any income they receive, which is deductible by the contributor, is exempt income to the recipient charity. To be exempt from taxation of its income, the charitable entity must be qualified under Section 501 of the Revenue Code.

Section 501 is titled: **Exemption from Tax on Corporations, Certain Trusts, Etc.** Not all entities covered by Section 501 are classed as "charitable." Those that are so classified are expressly identified in Subsection 501(c): List of Exempt Organizations. This subsection lists 26 different types of exempt entities. Those primarily identified as charitable are listed in subsection **501(c)(3)**, as referenced by Section 170(c): *Charitable Contribution Defined.*

Blended excerpts from Sections 170(c) and 501(c)(3) read as follows:

The term "charitable contributions" means a contribution or gift to or for the use of—

(i)   any corporation, trust, or community chest, fund, or foundation [which is]

(ii)   organized and operated exclusively for religious, charitable, scientific, testing for public safety, literary, or educational purposes, or to foster amateur sports competition, or for the prevention of cruelty to children or animals, or for veterans organizations, or for other exclusively public purposes [and]

(iii)   no part of the net earnings of which inures to the benefit of any private shareholder or individual [and]

(iv)   which is not engaged in carrying on propaganda, or attempting to influence legislation, or participating in any political campaign on behalf of any candidate for public office.

We're quoting these rather lengthy excerpts in order to familiarize you with the essentials of what constitutes a bona fide charitable contribution. As a trustee, you have a duty to make informed inquiry into the charitable activities of your intended donee organization. Insist on being given the specific tax code section, subsection, and subsubsection under which the entity is qualified. Also request its tax-exempt ID number. Not all beneficiaries of the trust may approve your choice of a charity. Consequently, you want to be prepared. Some beneficiaries may resent any of the trust's income going to charity, when they have a dire need for the income themselves.

Applicability of Schedule A (1041)

Ordinarily, a simple trust does not claim a charitable deduction. This is because the trust instrument, either by statement or implication, requires that all or most of the net income generated be distributed to living beneficiaries. In some cases, though, the instrument may provide the trustee with discretionary powers to make certain limited contributions The limitations are based on some "not to exceed" specified percentage of current income, or on the express desires of one or more beneficiaries (in memory of a deceased beneficiary).

Complex trusts, of the charitable remainder type, are required — mandated — to set aside certain amounts of current income (and current corpus) for charitable remainder purposes. The "charitable remainder" is established by actuarial factors of life expectancy of specific beneficiaries. The overall effect is that the designated beneficiary gets an income for life from the trust, part of which is taxable and part of which is nontaxable. The applicable tax rules for accomplishing this are very complicated. Recourse to Section 642(c) and its voluminous regulations is required. This section is titled: *Deduction for Amounts Paid or Permanently Set Aside for a Charitable Purpose*. The amount of deduction by the trust in a given year is unlimited, so long as the total accumulation of prior year set asides computationally meets the actuarial fraction required. Furthermore, the remainder contribution may be made to either a domestic or foreign charity.

A synopsis of deduction computations required (exclusive of actuarial factors) is presented in Figure 8.2. Note that the listed line entries are designated as Schedule A (1041). This is a preprinted schedule at the top of page 2 of Form 1041 titled: *Charitable Deduction*. A headnote to this preprinted schedule says—

Do not complete for a simple trust.

```
┌─────────────────────────────────────────────────────────┐
│ Schedule A (1041)        CHARITABLE DEDUCTION            │
├─────────────────────────────────────────────────────────┤
│   1. Amounts paid currently              _____     │
│   2. Amounts permanently set aside       _____     │
│   3. ADD lines 1 and 2                   _____     │
│   4. Allocable tax-exempt income         <_____>       │
│   5. SUBTRACT line 4 from line 3         _____     │
│   6. Capital gains paid or set aside     _____     │
│   7. ADD lines 4 and 5            ───▶  [_____]      │
│ ........................................................│
│         ENTER HERE AND ON PAGE 1 OF FORM 1041           │
└─────────────────────────────────────────────────────────┘
```

Fig. 8.2 - Entries Required for Computing Charitable Deduction

In addition, the official instructions say—

> *Trusts that claim a charitable deduction* [under Section 642(c)] *must also file Form 1041-A* [U.S. Information Return; Trust Accumulation of Charitable Amounts].

The principal item that we want to call to your attention in Figure 8.2 is line 4. It is labeled: *Tax-exempt income allocable to charitable contributions.* Because the beneficiaries who share in the charitable remainder interests get a tax benefit, the trust deduction has to be reduced allocably. For determining the amount of this reduction, the instructions at line 4 say—

> *Multiply line 3 by a fraction, the numerator of which is the total tax-exempt income of the trust, and the denominator of which is the gross income of the trust. Do not include in the denominator any losses allocated to corpus.*

The term "gross income" includes taxable and tax-exempt income combined. The same fraction: Total tax-exempt income divided by total gross income, is applied to other deductible expenditures of the trust which benefit the tax-exempt income. The whole idea of this allocation process is to prevent tax-exempt from getting a free ride on those deductions which otherwise directly reduce taxable income.

Legal & Accounting Fees

There is one class of expense deductions which may well benefit tax-exempt income along with taxable income. We have in mind those professional fees paid to attorneys, accountants, and tax return preparers. The generation of tax-exempt income is a highly passive affair, usually for the long term. As such, any attorney's attention is nil, an accountant's attention is minimal, and a return preparer's attention focuses on the allocable fraction of the deductible expenses on page 1 of Form 1041.

Ideally, professional consultants should indicate on their fee statement what portion or dollar amount of their fees is allocable to the tax-exempt income of the trust. An alert trustee should specifically request that this be done. If it is not done at the time of each fee statement submission, the IRS **presumes** the allocation to be proportional to the ratio of exempt income to gross income (which includes the exempt amount).

Deductible legal fees are those which apply to the trust administration process overall. This usually involves dispute letters, contract interpretation, and probate-type court proceedings. Some creditor or injured party may have a claim against the trust. The titling and ownership of trust property may be unclear. There may be a conflict of interest between two or more beneficiaries. Or, the trustee may be under attack for some perceived malfeasance of duty. Where legal fees relate to specific property holdings, such as rental real estate involving the eviction of tenants and processing of insurance claims, those fees attach directly to the income and expense accounting of the property itself.

Bookkeeping and accounting fees that relate to specific business activities are part of the expenses attributable to those activities. Examples are the preparation of income and expense spreadsheets (weekly, monthly, quarterly) for Schedules C (proprietorships), E-I (real estate rentals), E-II (partnerships and S corporations), and F (farm income or loss). These fees are deductible directly on said schedules rather than on Form 1041. However, if some "certified" accounting of the overall receipts and disbursements of the trust is required, the fees paid would be a 1041 item. Except for unusual circumstances, most trustees themselves do the banking, investing, checkwriting, and other general accounting chores.

Probably the most straightforward 1041 fee deductions are payments to tax return preparers. Form 1041 and all of its required attachments are prepared once a year. The effort includes all corresponding forms and schedules for instate and outstate filings. Said fees also include the preparation of information returns (W-2s, 1099s, K-1s, etc.); the preparation for and representation at IRS audits and appeals; and as a witness in Tax Court proceedings.

Investment advisory fees, property appraisal fees, financial counseling fees, and business consultation fees, are deductible elsewhere. They are *not* deductible as attorney, accountant, and return preparer fees. Property appraisals add to the cost basis of the property appraised. Business consulting fees are deductible on Schedules C, E, or F. Investment advisory and financial counseling fees are deductible as miscellaneous expenses under the 2% floor.

The "where" of professional fee deductions can be perplexing. Particularly so, if you are overly dependent on professionals and you allow them to run your affairs for you. Nevertheless, Figure 8.3 is intended as a helpful guideline to you when the fees become unavoidably pervasive.

Other Deductions Not Subject

The term "not subject" refers to the 2% floor that we mentioned earlier in this chapter. There are two categories of deductible expenditures on Form 1041 that reference the 2% floor. One category is NOT subject to the floor; the second category is SUBJECT to the floor. First, the not-subject category.

The instructions for the not-subject deductions say—

*Attach your own schedule, listing the type and amount, of all allowable deductions **not deductible elsewhere** on Form 1041.*

Do not include any losses on worthless bonds and similar obligations and nonbusiness bad debts. Report these losses on Schedule D (1041).

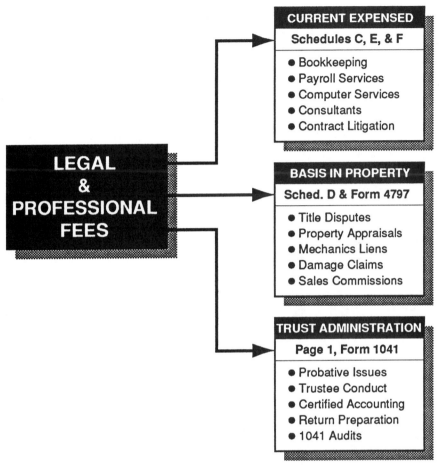

Fig. 8.3 - Caution When Assigning Professional Fees as Expenses

Other types of losses by the trust are deductible. These include:

- Casualty and theft loss (use Form 4684 to figure the losses)
- Net operating losses (use Form 1045: Schedule A, to figure the losses)
- Legal judgments against the trust (if any)

If the trust is a participant in partnership, S corporation, estate, or other trust, and there are pass-through items of amortization, depreciation, and depletion, they are deductible as not-subject expenses. All other items that pass through from these entities, for which no applicable preprinted line appears on the attachments to Form 1041, are also deductible here.

The general "not subject" rule (to the 2% floor) is Section 67(e)(1): *Determination of Adjusted Gross Income in Case of Trusts.* This rule reads in essential part that—

The deduction for costs which are paid or incurred in connection with the administration of the trust and which would not have been incurred if the property were not held in such trust . . .

are deductible without regard to the 2% floor.

Think of a trust as a quasi-business. It is not a for-profit business in the everyday operational sense of corporations, partnerships, and proprietorships. Yet, certain expenses are incurred strictly because it is a trust. Such expenses would be those necessary for inventorying, appraising, safekeeping, and rearranging of trust assets, overall. The trust is a "bundle of assets" which are to be protected irrespective of the 2% floor.

Determining the 2% Floor

The 2% floor is defined as: *2 percent of adjusted gross income* (AGI). In the case of a trust, there is a problem in establishing the AGI. Unlike an individual's 1040 return, there is no preprinted line labeled: *This is your adjusted gross income,* on a trust's 1041 return. So, what do you do? Unfortunately, Congress left it up to the IRS to figure out what to do.

The official instructions by the IRS for determining a trust's AGI are incomprehensible. But, if you like the challenge of computational reiterations, we refer you to the 1041 instructions at the section headed: *Allowable Miscellaneous Itemized Deductions Subject to the 2% Floor.* In these instructions, you will find a formula which reads like this—

AGI =   Total income (of the trust)
        MINUS the sum of

(a) fiduciary fees,
(b) attorney, accountant, and preparer fees,
(c) deductions not subject to the 2% floor,
(d) income distribution deduction (IDD),
(e) personal exemption (for the trust).

The "personal exemption" of a trust is $300 for a simple trust and $100 for a complex trust. The 2% of these amounts is computationally negligible: $6 and $2 respectively. They can be ignored for trust AGI purposes.

The big unknown in the formula above is the IDD (income distribution deduction). It is *the smaller of* the amount actually distributed to the beneficiaries or the DNI (distributable net income). Neither one can be computed precisely until the ATI (adjusted total income) of the trust is known. The ATI cannot be determined until the 2% floor amount is known. The 2% floor cannot be established until the AGI is known. The whole process is a round robin affair.

Our suggestion is that you use the formula above and **estimate** the IDD amount. Do this by rearranging the formula to—

IDD = Total income − [(a) + (b) + (c)]

This will give you a tentative amount. Round this amount *down* to the nearest $1,000 and let it go at that. After all, 2% of $1,000 is just $20. Realistically, you can't get much closer than this for trust accounting purposes. Hence, we schematize this estimating process for you in Figure 8.4.

If you persisted in establishing the precise IDD, technically, at least for a simple trust, you could reduce the trust AGI to virtually zero. A 2% of zero would be zero. Realizing this, why not just estimate the trust AGI at some round-number figure. Start with $1,000 and *increase* it by $500 "gut feel" increments for complex trusts accumulating income for distributions later.

The 1041 instructions conclude the 2% floor discourse by stating that—

If the 2% floor is more than the deductions subject to the 2% floor, no [such] *deductions are allowed.*

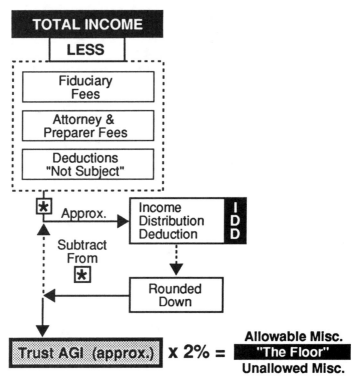

Fig. 8.4 - Technique for Estimating Trust AGI for 2% Floor Purposes

Expenses Affected by 2% Floor

Restating the above, the 2% floor is 0.02 x AGI of the trust. Assuming an AGI of $10,000, for example, the "floor" is $200 (0.02 x 10,000). This means that the aggregate of all miscellaneous expenses above $200 is deductible. If the aggregate is $200 or less, the expenses are not deductible.

What are the kinds of expenses that are subject to the 2% floor?

The following list covers most of the affected miscellaneous-type expenses:

(1) Travel and lodging,
(2) Meals and entertainment,
(3) Office-type expenses and supplies,
(4) Office-type furnishings and equipment,

(5) Office rent and repairs,
(6) Postage and shipping costs,
(7) Auto leasing and operating expenses,
(8) Dues, subscriptions, and publications,
(9) Document preparation and certification fees,
(10) Phone, utilities, and faxes,
(11) Investment advisory fees,
(12) Educational-type seminars, and

. . . "anything else" that is not specifically allowed as a deduction under other sections of the Tax Code.

Because of the difficulty in precisely computing the 2% AGI for trusts, Congress in 1988 granted the IRS certain "legislative grace." In its Committee Report P.L. 100-647, Congress pointed out that—

*Under Section 67(e), the [IRS] has regulatory authority to apply the two-percent floor **at the beneficiary level**, rather than at the entity level, with respect to trusts required to distribute income currently.* [Emphasis added.]

In other words, when there is significant doubt about the 2% floor, you have the discretion to pass the above listed expenses allocably through to the beneficiaries. At the beneficiary level, computing the 2% AGI is quite straightforward. However, most beneficiaries would get little or no deduction benefit from these passthroughs. This is because their AGI would include other sources of income which did not arise from the trust.

Our experience has been that, except for "subject to" expenses exceeding 10% of the total income of the trust, estimating the trust's AGI is good enough. The amount of estimate should, of course, be stated on the Form 1041 return. But even if your estimate is off substantially from the precise AGI figure, the resulting effect on the adjusted total income of the trust would be minimal.

Adjusted Total Income

Altogether, there are seven categories of administrative deductions allowed against the total income of the trust. We listed these deductions earlier in our "overview." Because all such deductions are important adjustments to total income, we relist them here for summary purposes:

1. Interest,
2. Taxes,
3. Fiduciary fees,
4. Charitable deduction,
5. Attorney, accountant, and return preparer fees,
6. Other deductions NOT subject to 2% floor, and
7. Miscellaneous deductions SUBJECT to 2% floor.

Preferably, a separate listing should be attached to Form 1041 itemizing the deductions claimed. This is particularly true for categories 6 and 7, which beneficiaries would rarely understand.

All administrative deductions are totaled, then subtracted from the total (tax accountable) income of the trust. The result is—

Adjusted total income or (loss).

The specific instructions at this point read:

If the amount is a loss that is attributable wholly or in part to the capital loss limitation rules, then enter as a negative amount the smaller of the [adjusted total income] *or the amount of capital loss* [included in the total income]. *If the* [adjusted total income] *is not attributable to any capital loss, enter zero.*

Special rules apply when there are capital gains and losses resulting from transactional activities, and when there is distributable tax-exempt income. We'll touch on these rules in the next two chapters.

Meanwhile, if the adjusted total income is zero, there is no taxable income to be distributed to the beneficiaries. There may be some nontaxable distributions, however.

9

THE DISTRIBUTION DEDUCTION

All Gratuitous Trusts Enjoy One Dominant Deduction: The "Income Distribution Deduction" (IDD). Said Amount Is Limited By DISTRIBUTABLE NET INCOME (DNI) Which Is The Transference Of Taxable Income From The Trust To The Beneficiaries. The Precise Amount Of IDD Allowed Involves A 17-Step Computational Process Which Identifies Separately (a) Income REQUIRED To Be Distributed, (b) Tax-Exempt Income, (c) Capital Gain Distributions, (d) "Property-In-Kind" Distributions, And (e) "Set Asides" For Charity. All 17 Steps Are Required For Complex Trusts; Fewer For Simple Trusts. That Which Is Distributed Is Not Taxed In The Trust.

The term "deduction" means a subtraction against the tax-accountable income of the trust. Said income is that dollar amount which exists at the line designated as *Adjusted total income* (ATI) on page 1 of Form 1041. If you recall from Chapters 7 and 8, you are aware that the tax-exempt income plays no direct role in determining the ATI. It does, however, play an indirect role by reducing the allowable administrative deductions for those deduction expenditures which are attributable to the generation of tax-exempt income. Whether such income is taxable or not, it must bear its own share of expenses.

If there were no further deductions allowed on Form 1041, the ATI would become the taxable income of the trust. But this is not the case. Before arriving at the true taxable income, three other distributive-type deductions are allowed. These are:

1. Income distribution deduction
2. Estate tax deduction (rarely applicable)
3. Exemption deduction ($300 simple; $100 complex)

Of these three, the dominant one is the **Income distribution deduction** (IDD). This is the computational deduction allowed for distributions of tax-accountable income to one or more beneficiaries of the trust. In simple trusts, particularly, this one deduction alone can eliminate all taxes on the trust. In complex trusts, the IDD can reduce substantially the trust's taxable income. It is for these reasons that we title this chapter: THE Distribution Deduction. The term "the," however, refers exclusively to *income*: **not** to corpus.

Establishing the amount of IDD allowable is a 17-step process. The process requires accounting for tax-exempt income, capital gains and losses, charitable deductions and set asides, and requirements imposed by the trust instrument and applicable local law. The computations are much simplified for simple trusts. Consequently, we want to explore more fully the tax law distinctions between simple and complex trusts. Then we'll step you through the IDD computational schedule. This schedule appears on page 2 of Form 1041, and is designated as **Schedule B**: Income Distribution Deduction.

Simple Trust Defined

Section 651 of the Internal Revenue Code addresses the definitional aspects of simple trusts. This section is officially titled: *Deduction for Trusts Distributing Current Income Only*. Note that the term "simple trust" does not appear in this title. This is because the focus stress is on "distributing current income only."

More directly, Regulation 1.651(a)-1: *Simple trusts*, describes such trusts as those whose "governing instrument" provides that—

(1) all of its income be distributed currently;
(2) no charitable contribution be made; and
(3) no distributions from corpus be made.

Regulation 1.651(a)-1(b) goes on to say—

*A trust may be a simple trust for one year and a complex trust for another year. . . . Under Section 651 a trust qualifies as a simple trust in a taxable year in which it is **required** to distribute all of its income currently . . . **whether or not** the distributions of current income are in fact made.* [Emphasis added.]

What income is *required* to be distributed currently?

The answer depends on the terms of the trust instrument and the applicable local law. For example, Regulation 1.651(a)-2 points out that—

If the trust instrument provides that the trustee in determining the distributable income shall first retain a reserve for depreciation or otherwise make due allowance for keeping the trust corpus intact by retaining a reasonable amount of current income for that purpose, the retention of current income for that purpose will not disqualify the trust from being a "simple" trust. . . . It is immaterial, for purposes of determining whether all the income is required to be distributed currently, that the amount of income allocated to a particular beneficiary is not specified in the instrument.

Regulation 1.651(a)-3: *Distribution of amounts other than income*, makes it clear that—

A trust does not qualify for treatment [as a simple trust] *for any taxable year in which it actually distributes corpus. . . . A trust, otherwise qualifying* [as a simple trust], *which may make a distribution of corpus in the discretion of the trustee, or which is required under the terms of its governing instrument to make a distribution of corpus upon the happening of a specific event, will be disqualified for treatment under section 651 only for the taxable year in which an actual distribution of corpus is made.*

The idea behind a simple trust is that, some day, the trust will terminate. In anticipation of such event, all variants of income generated in the meantime should be distributed annually. This is so that, in a strictly theoretical sense, the initial corpus of the trust would remain undiminished — and unenhanced — until the trust instrument directs otherwise.

Section 661: Complex Trusts

The official title of Section 661 is: *Deduction for Trusts Accumulating Income or Distributing Corpus.* Though the term "complex trust" does not appear in this title, it is implied in the terms "accumulating income" and "distributing corpus." In addition, a complex trust can contribute income, corpus, or a combination of both to charity.

The essence of Section 661 is its subsection (a): *Deduction.* This subsection reads in principal part—

In any taxable year there shall be allowed as a deduction in computing taxable income of a trust (other than a [simple] *trust), the sum of—*

(1) any amount of income . . . required to be distributed currently (including any amount required to be distributed which may be paid out of income or corpus . . .); and

(2) any other amounts properly paid or credited or required to be distributed for such taxable year; but such deduction shall not exceed the distributable net income of the trust. [Emphasis added.]

From the above citation, you can sense immediately that a complex trust can do far more things than a simple trust. For this greater latitude, though, the clause "shall not exceed" implies greater computational complexity. Indeed it does. When we get to the 17-step computational sequence for the amount of deduction allowed, you'll see what we mean.

In the meantime, we present in Figure 9.1 a bird's eye view of the distributive differences between a simple trust and a complex trust. A point to keep in mind is that a complex trust can always do what a simple trust can do . . . but **not** vice versa. However, for

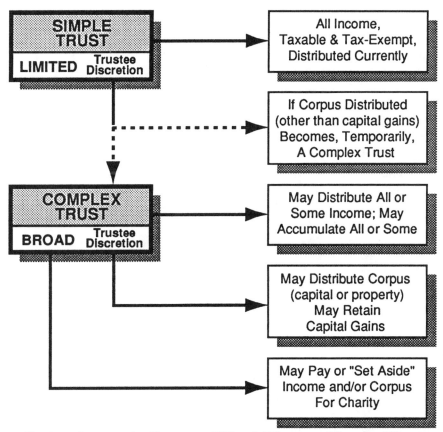

Fig. 9.1 - Comparative Features of "Simple" Trust vs. "Complex" Trust

specific events, a simple trust can self-convert to a complex trust for a particular year, then revert back to a simple trust thereafter.

Character of Amounts Distributed

Both simple and complex trusts have to "characterize" their distributions in proportion to the origin of the income source within the trust. This is called the *proration rule*. The idea is to prevent the trustee from shifting tax-exempt income to high-bracket beneficiaries, while paying out taxable income to lower-income beneficiaries. If different amounts and classes are specifically allocated to designated beneficiaries pursuant to the trust instrument and local law, then each beneficiary is deemed to have received the items specifically allocated. Any such special allocation, however must have an economic effect independent of tax consequences.

In view of the above, it should be self-evident that the proration procedures are more complex for complex trusts than for simple trusts. Indeed, such is the case.

As substantiation of such fact, Section 661(b): *Character of Amounts Distributed*, reads in part as follows:

> *The amount* [of deduction] . . . *shall be treated as consisting of the same proportion of each class of items entering into the computation of distributable income . . . as the total of each class bears to the total distributable income of the trust, in the absence of the allocation of different classes of income under the specific terms of the governing instrument.* [Emphasis added.]

The best way to illustrate the significance of Section 661(b) is by a numerical example (using simple numbers). Consider that a trust generates $40,000 of income from three sources, namely: Rents $20,000; Taxable interest $10,000; and Tax-exempt interest: $10,000. From this total, the trustee pays $3,000 to charity; $2,000 for rental expenses; and $2,000 in fiduciary fees. After which, the trustee distributes $16,500 to the beneficiaries (and, within his discretion, *accumulates within the trust* the same amount). How is the distributed $16,500 characterized and prorated?

We display the results for you in Figure 9.2. Note that the charitable contribution is spread over all three income sources, proportionately. The rental expenses, obviously, are assigned only to the rental income. The fiduciary fee is allocated to rental income and tax-exempt income because of the trustee's greater attention to these items than to taxable interest income.

IRS regulations 1.661(b)-1 and 1.661(c)-2 give greater detail than we have presented. Nevertheless, the general gist is as we have illustrated in Figure 9.2. The dollar amounts shown were intentionally chosen to illustrate that not all of available distributable net income is deemed distributed. For purposes of the distribution deduction for the trust, there are limitation rules that apply.

ITEM	Type of Income			
	Rental	Taxable	Tax-Exempt	TOTAL
Trust Income	$20,000	$10,000	$10,000	$40,000
LESS				
Rental Expenses	2,000	—	—	2,000
Fiduciary Fee	1,500		500	2,000
Charitable Contributions	1,500	750	750	3,000
Total Deductions	5,000	750	1,250	7,000
Distributable Net Income	15,000	9,250	8,750	33,000
AMOUNT DEEMED DISTRIBUTED	7,500	4,625	4,375	16,500

Fig. 9.2 - Example of "Character of Amounts Distributed" to a Beneficiary

Limitation on Deduction

Section 651 (simple trusts) and Section 661 (complex trusts) both have a limitation imposed on the amount of distribution to beneficiaries that can be deducted from the taxable income of the trust. This is the consequence of the *matching principle* between the deductible income of the trust and the includible income of the beneficiaries. What the trust deducts, the beneficiaries must include. We try to illustrate this principle in Figure 9.3. The limitation mandate is addressed in subsection (b) of Section 651 and in subsection (c) of Section 661. Both subsections are subtitled: *Limitation on Deduction.*

Subsection 651(b) for simple trusts is more self-explanatory; hence, we cite it first. It reads in full as—

If the amount of income required to be distributed currently exceeds the distributable net income of the trust for the taxable year, the deduction **shall be limited** *to the amount of the* **distributable net income.** *For this purpose, the* **computation** *of the distributable income shall not include items of income which are not included in the gross income of the trust and the deductions allocable thereto.* [Emphasis added.]

This citation tells us three things. One: the limitation amount is based on *Distributable Net Income* Two: there is a computational process that must be pursued to establish the DNI. And, three: the computation excludes sources of income (such as tax-exempt interest) and deductions which are reflected in adjusted total income of the trust (such as charitable contributions).

In the case of complex trusts, the limitation mandate of subsection 661(c) reads (in part) as—

No [distribution] deduction shall be allowed . . . in respect of any portion . . . which is treated . . . as consisting of any item of **distributable net income** *which is not included in the gross income of the trust.*

In complex trusts, the DNI computation involves adjustments for charitable contributions, deductions allocable to tax-exempt interest, capital gains, capital losses, and prior income accumulations, allocations to corpus, and income from foreign trusts. These adjustments are prescribed by Section 643(a): **Distributable Net Income Defined.** We believe that Figure 9.3 is more helpful than our trying to cite to you the wording in Section 643(a). The computational sequence below is intended to augment the concept in Figure 9.3.

Regulation 1.643(a)-0 is helpful to the extent that it states that—

The term "distributable net income" has no application except in the taxation of trusts and their beneficiaries. It limits the deductions allowable to trusts for amounts paid, credited, or required to be distributed to beneficiaries and is used to determine how much of an amount paid, credited, or required to be distributed to a beneficiary will be includible in his gross income. It is also used to determine the character of distributions to the beneficiaries.

DNI Computational Sequence

Functionally, the DNI (distributable net income) is strictly a reference amount. It is a *limitation* amount. To determine the DNI,

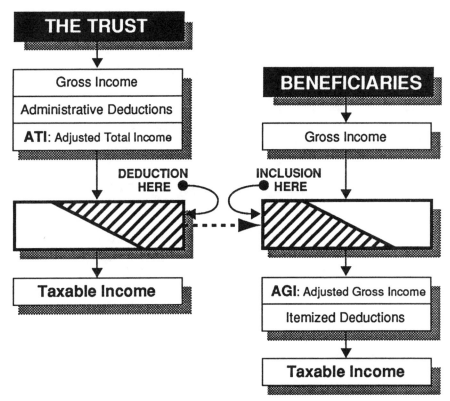

Fig. 9.3 - The "Transfer" of Taxable Income from a Trust to its Beneficiaries

a total of nine summary-type computational steps is required. Each is a "summary type" in the sense that separate adjustments for each step are required. Necessarily, these adjustments add complexity of their own. The nine DNI steps are the first in a sequence of 17 steps for arriving at the IDD (income distribution deduction) for the trust. All 17 steps appear as "Schedule B" on page 2 of Form 1041.

The nine DNI computational steps are presented in Figure 9.4. As you can see, Step 1 is the adjusted total income (ATI) of the trust. It is transferred directly from page 1 of Form 1041 to page 2, where it is subject to further adjustments. The official wording at Step 1 adds: "See instructions."

The Step 1 instructions point out that if the ATI is a loss, you (as trustee) must examine the character of the loss. If it is attributable in whole or part to the capital loss limitation rule of $3,000 per year,

Sched. B	INCOME DISTRIBUTION DEDUCTION	Form 1041
1	Adjusted total income _____	
2	Adjusted tax-exempt interest _____	
3	Total net gain from Sch. D (1041) _____	
4	Capital gain allocated to charity _____	
5	Long term gain set aside for charity _____	
6	Short term gain set aside for charity _____	
7	If capital loss on page 1, enter as positive _____	
8	If capital gain on page 1, enter as negative _____	
9	**DNI** Combine steps 1 through 8 • If zero or less, enter -0- ▶	⬚

To Be Continued

Fig. 9.4 - The 9 Steps for Arriving at DNI on Form 1041

you enter the smaller of the ATI loss or $3,000 as a negative amount at Step 1. If the ATI loss is not attributable to any capital loss — called "ordinary loss" — you enter zero. The idea here is that a capital loss affects corpus, whereas an ordinary loss affects income.

Still further, the Step 1 instructions tell you that if the amount of dividends in the page 1 gross income includes extraordinary dividends, another adjustment to ATI is required. An "extra-ordinary dividend" is one which exceeds 10% of the trust's tax basis in that particular dividend-paying stock. Such excess payments become nontaxable return of capital to the corpus of the trust. The trust's basis in that stock must be decreased correspondingly. This also means that the ATI must be reduced similarly. The term "dividends" on page 1 of the 1041 means *ordinary* dividends only. Therefore, extraordinary dividends — because they are return of capital: nontaxable — are not classed as income.

Adjusted Tax-Exempt Income

For DNI purposes, tax-exempt income is included in the computational process. Here, the term "income" includes tax-exempt *interest* and/or tax-exempt *dividends*. The idea for this inclusion is that exempt interest-dividend income is all part of the money pot that is available for distribution to beneficiaries and to charities. After certain "adjustments" are made to the exempt income, the net amount becomes Step 2 in Figure 9.4.

There are three adjustments (subtractions) from tax-exempt income. They are:

1. Amount of tax-exempt income allocable to charitable contributions (if any),

2. Allocable portion of total income-producing expenses attributable to both taxable and tax-exempt income, and

3. Interest expense directly attributable to the acquisition of tax-exempt securities.

These adjustments are mandated by IRS Regulation 1.643(a)-5(a): *Tax-exempt interest.* This regulation reads in part as—

There is included in distributable net income any tax-exempt interest excluded from gross income under section 103 [interest on state and local bonds], ***reduced by*** *disbursements* ***allocable to*** *. . . section 265* [expenses and interest for tax-exempt income] *. . . and section 642* [special rules . . . for charitable purposes]. [Emphasis added.]

As you can sense from this regulation, the inclusion of tax-exempt income may increase — or, it may decrease — the DNI computational base. Steps 1 and 2 are the "starting points" before the DNI is known. There are still Steps 3 through 8 to be pursued.

Capital Gains & Losses

Steps 1 and 2 represent what we class as the "ordinary income" aspects of trust activities. In contrast, Steps 3 through 8 represent the "capital transactions" of the trust. Capital transactions involve the sale, exchange, or other transformation of corpus assets. Every capital transaction results in either a capital gain, return of capital, or capital loss. Ordinarily, capital transaction results are *excluded* from the concept of DNI: distributable net income. Corpus/capital changes ordinarily remain in the trust; they are not distributed unless the trust instrument or local law requires their distribution. The moment any capital amount is actually distributed, all capital gains and losses (for a given year) **are** included in the DNI computation. This is the role of Steps 3 through 8 in Figure 9.4.

Regulation 1.643(a)-3: *Capital gains and losses*, makes the exclusion-inclusion point clear. Its subregulation (a) reads as—

Except [with respect to foreign trusts], *gains from the sale or exchange of capital assets are* **ordinarily excluded** *from distributable net income and are ordinarily not considered as paid, credited, or required to be distributed to any beneficiary unless they are:*

(1) Allocated to income under the terms of the governing instrument or local law by the fiduciary on its books or **by** *notice to the beneficiary,*

(2) Allocated to corpus and **actually distributed** *to beneficiaries during the taxable year, or*

(3) **Utilized (pursuant** *to the terms of the governing instrument or the* **practice followed by the fiduciary)** *in determining the amount which is distributed or required to be distributed.* [Emphasis added.]

If capital gains are paid, set aside, or used for charitable purposes, said gains must be included in the DNI computation. Generally, capital losses are excluded except to the extent that they enter into the determination of includible capital gains. Any capital gains or losses retained in trust and not actually distributed to beneficiaries are excluded from the DNI computation.

The Capital Inclusion Steps

In Figure 9.4, we presented an abbreviated description of Steps 3 through 8. Let's now expand on these descriptions and see if the rationale for capital inclusions in the DNI make sense.

Step 3 reads officially as—

Total net gain from Schedule D (Form 1041), line 17, column (a). See instructions.

Schedule D (1041) is titled: **Capital Gains and Losses.** Line 17 is titled: **Total net gain or loss.** Column (a) is titled: **Beneficiaries.** The instructions to column (a): **Beneficiaries' Allocation**, read in part—

*Enter the amount of net gain or loss allocable to the beneficiary or beneficiaries. Except in the final year, include only those losses that are taken into account in determining the amount of **gain** from the sale or exchange of capital assets that is **paid, credited, or required** to be distributed to any beneficiary during the tax year.* [Emphasis added.]

The term "any beneficiary," by the way, does **not** include distributions for charitable purposes. Step 3, therefore, is strictly for capital distributions to beneficiaries.

Step 4, as well as steps 5 and 6, address capital distributions for charitable purposes. Step 4 reads officially as—

Enter the amount from Schedule A, line 6.

Schedule A (1041) is titled: **Charitable Deduction.** Its line 6 is titled: *Capital gains for the tax year **allocated to corpus and paid or permanently set aside for charitable purposes.*** The term "allocated to corpus" is column (b) of Schedule D (1041), line 17. This column is headed: *Trust's* (allocation). Obviously, only capital gains can be paid or set aside by the trust for charitable purposes. No charity wants capital losses assigned to it. The reason, obviously, is that charities are tax-exempt entities. Any otherwise tax benefit of capital loss pass-throughs is meaningless.

Steps 5 and 6 segregate short-term (1 year or less) and long-term (more than 1 year) capital gains from each other. This segregation eliminates capital losses from the total netting process. These steps read officially as—

5. *Long-term capital gain for the tax year included on Schedule A, line 3.*

6. *Short-term capital gain for the tax year included on Schedule A, line 3.*

Line 3 of Schedule A pertains to amounts paid or set aside from gross income for charitable purposes. The term "gross income," recall, includes ordinary income or loss, as well as capital gain or loss. For each of Steps 5 and 6, you have to separate out the capital gain portions. This separation is necessary in order to establish whether the capital gain is to be treated as addition to corpus . . . or as addition to income.

Steps 7 and 8 comprise additional effort to segregate capital gains and capital losses from the gross income on page 1 of Form 1041. These lines read:

7. *If the amount on page 1, line 4 is a capital loss, enter here as a **positive** figure.*

8. *If the amount on page 1, line 4, is a capital gain, enter here as a **negative** figure.*

Line 4 on page 1 of Form 1041 is titled: **Capital gain or loss. Attach Schedule D (Form 1041).**

By entering at Step 7 the line 4 capital loss as a positive figure, the DNI computation recognizes that said loss "eats into" the trust corpus, thereby making that amount available for distribution to beneficiaries.

By entering at Step 8 the line 4 capital gain as a negative figure, the DNI is reduced back to its basic tenet of being distributable *ordinary income* . . . to the beneficiaries. Any component of the capital gain which goes to charity is automatically "backed out" by means of Schedule D: column (b) for charity and column (a) for beneficiaries. Computationally, Step 8 is a brilliant move for separating ordinary income from capital gain, when making taxable distributions to the beneficiaries.

If DNI Zero: Stop

Step 9 in Figure 9.4 — **DNI** — reads exactly as the words appear officially on Form 1041, namely:

Combine lines [steps] *1 through 8. If zero or less, enter -0-.*

Here, the term "combine" means that you combine all of the positive and negative amounts in Steps 1 through 8. If the result is zero or less (meaning: negative), you must enter zero. This is because there can be no negative DNI amount.

Keep in mind that the DNI represents distributable ordinary income only. It does not even represent distributable capital gains to the beneficiaries. (Capital gains are passed through independently of ordinary income: more on this in upcoming Chapter 10.) Except in the final year of the trust, no ordinary loss — nor capital loss, for that matter — can be passed through to the beneficiaries. Therefore, should the DNI amount at step 9 be zero, there is no qualified distributable deduction for the trust.

In other words, the DNI routine is the "testing ground" for determining whether there is any current-year income to be distributed. If not, because of set asides, the trust itself may be taxed whereas the beneficiaries would not. From this point on, any continuation of Schedule B would be meaningless. In most cases, however, the DNI is generally positive.

Whatever appears at Step 9 as the DNI is a reference amount only. It is the maximum amount distributable. Often, a lesser amount qualifies as the distribution deduction for the trust. This is why Steps 10 through 16 are required. For example, if the DNI is $20,000 and Steps 10 through 16 produce an amount of $15,000, the income distribution deduction (IDD) allowable is the $15,000.

Continuation Beyond DNI

Steps 10 through 17 (IDD) are presented in abbreviated form in Figure 9.5. A quick glance at these steps reveals that no capital gains are involved. However, there are five variant forms of income characterized sequentially as follows:

9	**DNI** Combine steps 1 through 8 ▶	
10	Accounting income, if complex trust - - - - - - - - - - - - - - -	
11	Income required distributed currently - - - - - - - - - - - - - -	
12	Other amounts paid, etc. -	
13	Total distributions. Add steps 11 and 12. If greater than 10, see instructions.	
14	Tax-exempt income in step 13 - - - - - - - - - - - - - - - - - - -	
15	Tentative 1. Subtract 14 from 13 - - - - - - - - - - - - - - - - -	
16	Tentative 2. Subtract 2 from 9 - - - - - - - - - - - - - - - - - - -	
17	**IDD** INCOME DISTRIBUTION DEDUCTION Enter the SMALLER OF step 15 or step 16	

Fig. 9.5 - Continuation of Schedule B (1041) for Arriving at IDD

Accounting income: Step 10
Current required income: Step 11
Other amounts paid, etc.: Step 12
Prior accumulations of income: Step 13
Tax-exempt income: Step 14

A further descriptive word or two on each of these steps is in order.

With regard to Step 10: *Accounting Income*, the instructions say—

> *If you are filing for a **simple trust, skip this line.** If you are filing for a complex trust, enter the income determined under the terms of the governing instrument and applicable local law. Do not include extraordinary dividends or taxable stock dividends . . . allocable to corpus.*

In other words, "accounting income" is whatever the trust instrument says it is, other than amounts set aside for charitable purposes. It includes all forms of income for which the trustee has to make an accounting to the beneficiaries, whether distributed, distributable, or not.

Step 11 is: *Income Required to be Distributed Currently*. The instructions require that an entry—

*Be completed by all simple trusts as well as complex trusts, that are **required** to distribute income currently, whether it is distributed or not.*

Step 12: ***Other Amounts Paid, Etc.***, is to be completed ONLY for complex trusts. The instructions go on to say—

These [items] consist of any other amounts paid, credited, or required to be distributed and are referred to as "second tier" distributions. Such amounts include annuities to the extent not paid out of income, discretionary distributions of corpus, and distributions of property in kind.

The term "other amounts" also includes tax-exempt income.

Step 13: ***Total Distributions***, officially reads—

*Add lines [steps] 11 and 12. If greater than line [step] 10, see [specific] instructions . . . [for completion of Schedule J (1041): **Accumulation Distribution for a Complex Trust**].*

Schedule J is for complex trusts only. It is predicated upon the *throwback principle* for *retaxing* the prior accumulations of undistributed income. For each throwback year, there are some **35** computational steps for arriving at a tax imposed on the cumulative undistributed net income. The idea is to discourage accumulations within the trust as a tax deferment device for its beneficiaries.

Step 14: ***Tax-Exempt Income***, officially reads—

Enter the amount of tax-exempt income included in Step 13.

The instructions accompanying Step 14 read—

In figuring the income distribution deduction, the trust is not allowed a deduction for any item of the DNI that is not included in the gross [tax accountable] income of the trust. Thus, for purposes of figuring the allowable income distribution deduction, the DNI is figured without regard to any tax-exempt income.

Use the "Smaller of"

Steps 15 and 16 are *tentative* distribution deductions. In Figure 9.5, we label them respectively as Tentative 1 (step 15) and Tentative 2 (step 16). They are "tentative" in the sense that either one may become the allowable distribution deduction for the trust.

The preprinted instructions directly on Schedule B (1041) for arriving at these tentative amounts are self-explanatory.

At this point, we have two tentative allowable distribution deductions. There is Step 15 (No. 1) and Step 16 (No. 2). Which of the two is allowable?

The allowable IDD amount is the very last entry on Schedule B (Form 1041). It is Step 17 back in Figure 9.5. It is bold captioned: *Income Distribution Deduction*, which is identical with the caption of Schedule B itself. The preprinted instructions thereon say—

Enter the smaller of line [step] *15 or line* [step] *16 here, and on page 1* [of Form 1041 at] *line* [Income distribution deduction].

The supplemental instructions for Step 17 read in principal part:

The income distribution deduction determines the amount of income that will be taxed to the beneficiaries.

There you have it! Whatever evolves as the bottom line on Schedule B becomes an allowable distribution deduction against the taxable income of the trust. The exact same amount is mandatorily included in the gross income of the beneficiaries. Where there is more than one beneficiary, the IDD is allocated to each beneficiary in proportion to his or her distributive share of the trust income.

10

THE BENEFICIARY K-1s

All Trust Income And Corpus Eventually Must Be Distributed To Beneficiaries. The Vehicle For Doing So Is Schedule K-1 ... Or "K-1" For Short. It focuses on 5 Classes Of Income, Namely: (1) Interest, (2) Dividends, (3) Capital Gain, (4) Nonpassive Income, And (5) Passive Income. Class (4) Denotes Significant Personal Participation By The Trustor Or Trustee In An Active Ongoing Business. Class (5) Denotes Occasional Decision-Making In An Activity Such As Rental Real Estate. Although There Are Deductions And Credits On A K-1, Most Apply To Complex Trusts Which Accumulate Income Or Distribute To Charity.

Schedule K-1 (Form 1041) is officially titled: *Beneficiary's Share of Income, Deductions, Credits, etc.* Note that this title is singular possessive: Beneficiary's. This implies that there is one Schedule K-1 for each separate beneficiary of a trust. Such, indeed, is the case. A headnote instruction on the K-1 says—

Complete a separate Schedule K-1 for each beneficiary.

The significance of this instruction is that each beneficiary's share is independent of that for all other beneficiaries. The word "complete" means making applicable entries in the 36 designated information lines on the K-1. Though there are many potential entries, rarely are more than six for any one beneficiary required. Which six? It all depends.

When each K-1 is completed, it is known as an "information" return. It is not a tax return, per se. As a trustee, you have no duty to prepare the tax returns of the beneficiaries. But, you do have a duty to furnish *tax information* to each beneficiary, AND to the IRS. Each beneficiary uses the K-1 information to prepare his or her own tax return. The IRS uses the information to computer-match what you have furnished with that which each beneficiary self-reports.

The cardinal rule for preparing each K-1 is to "characterize" the income and deduction entries thereon to correspond directly with those on page 1 of Form 1041. This is called the *character allocation* rule of Section 652 (for simple trusts) and of Section 662 (for complex trusts). Character allocations can become a formidable task when a trust has multiple sources of income, or diversity of administrative deductions, and more than one beneficiary.

As a consequence of the above, our focus in this chapter is to familiarize you with the format and contents of Schedule K-1, and the allocation rules relating thereto. We'll also give some numerical examples to help you grasp the pass-through concepts involved (from the trust to the beneficiary).

The Start-off Instructions

The instructions for preparing the K-1s are found in the Form 1041 instructions. For example, the instruction subheaded: *Schedule K-1; Who Must File*, reads—

The fiduciary (or one of the joint fiduciaries) must file Schedule K-1. A copy of each beneficiary's K-1 is attached to the Form 1041 filed with the IRS and each beneficiary is given a copy of his or her respective K-1. One copy of each Schedule K-1 must be retained for the fiduciary's records.

On the left headportion of each K-1 there is a half-page width block which reads—

Beneficiary's identifying number　　▶ _____
Beneficiary's name, address, and ZIP code.

A beneficiary's "identifying number" is, of course, his/her social security number (SSN). It is up to the trustee to request from each beneficiary his or her SSN, as well as his or her correct name, address, and ZIP code. As recipients of trust income — some of which is taxed and some not — most beneficiaries comply without the need for any formal demand.

There is another instructional reminder, subheaded: **Character of Income.** Its short one paragraph reads—

The beneficiary's income is considered to have the same portion of each class of items entering into the computation of DNI that the total of each class has to the DNI.

Let us illustrate this "character of income" with simple numbers. Suppose that the trust's DNI (distributable net income) is $32,000 for four equal-share beneficiaries (i.e., $8,000 each). Further, suppose that the total income of the trust consists of 30% interest, 25% dividends, and 45% capital gain. The $8,000 income distribution to each beneficiary is characterized as:

Interest	$2,400	($8,000 x 30%)
Dividends	2,000	(8,000 x 25%)
Cap. Gain	3,600	(8,000 x 45%)
	$8,000	

Yet, another important start-off instruction: **Gifts and Bequests,** reads—

Do not include in the beneficiary's income any gifts or bequests of a specific sum of money or specific property under the terms of the governing instrument that are paid or credited in three installments or less.

The premise here is that gifts and bequests are distributions of corpus: not of income. As such, corpus gifts and bequests are not taxable to the recipient(s). This is because the corpus assets were already taxed when they were transferred irrevocably to the trust.

With the above highlights in mind, we present in Figure 10.1 the general format and contents of Schedule K-1. For orientation purposes, we have numbered the entry-line groupings in an abbreviated manner unlike the 36 lines on an official K-1.

Form 1041	BENEFICIARY'S SHARE OF INCOME, ETC.		Tax Year of Trust
Beneficiary's SSN:	**Trust's EIN:**		
Beneficiary's name, address, zip	**Fiduciary's name, address, zip**		
(a) Allocable Share Item	**(b) Amount**		**(c) Where to Enter on Form 1040**
1. Portfolio income • Interest • Dividends • Cap.gain	$		Schedules B & D
2. Annuities, rents, etc. • Nonpassive income • Passive income	$		Schedule E and elsewhere
3. Minimum tax items	$		Form 6251
4. Special tax items • Estate tax deduction • Foreign tax paid	$		Schedule A Form 1116
5. Tax preference items • Depreciation • Depletion • Amortization	$		Form 6251 Form 8801
6. Final year deductions • Loss carryovers	$		Scheds. A & D Form 6251
7. Other items • Prepayment credits • Tax-exempt interest • Nontaxable items	$		On applicable lines of appropriate forms

Fig. 10.1 - Format and Groupings of "Allocable Share Items" on Sch. K-1

Section 652: Simple Trusts

Before actually tackling the entry-line groups on Schedule K-1, it is important to be apprised of the basic tax laws affecting beneficiaries. For simple trusts, this is Section 652. It is titled: *Inclusion of Amounts in Gross Income of Beneficiaries of Trusts Distributing Current Income Only*. This title is a statement in and of itself. It has three subsections: (a), (b), and (c).

The essence of subsection 652(a): *Inclusion*, is that all income "required" to be distributed shall be included in the gross income of the beneficiaries . . . *whether distributed or not.* The clause "whether . . . or not" does not grant the trustee any special discretionary powers to withhold distributable income. The clause simply means that the trustee can complete the accounting for the trust for its taxable year, before actually distributing the income. This avoids premature distributions and the possibility of excess distributions. Should there be distributions which exceed the DNI, all distributions shall be prorated to the extent of the DNI. Thereafter, any valid excess is treated as nontaxable distributions to the beneficiaries.

The essence of subsection 652(b): *Character of Amounts*, is that the character of the DNI in the hands of the beneficiaries shall be the same as in the hands of the trust. In other words, if the trust distributes its net rental income, the beneficiaries treat their prorata share also as net rental income. Where the trust instrument *specifically allocates* different classes of income to different beneficiaries, there must be a valid economic reason for doing so. The differentiation could specify those beneficiaries who are physically handicapped, minors, elderly, or innately economically disadvantaged. Otherwise, in simple trusts, particularly, the trustee has no discretionary authority to switch the classes of income around just to satisfy the tax peculiarities of different beneficiaries.

The essence of subsection (c): *Different Taxable Years*, is that the tax year of the trust is controlling. Therefore, if a beneficiary has a different tax year ending from that of the trust, he shall include the K-1 information which occurs . . . *within or with his taxable year.* The "within or with" rule applies to short tax years as well as to tax years of normal duration. If a beneficiary dies, only the amount actually distributed to him before his death is includible in gross income for his last (and final) 1040 tax year.

Section 662: Complex Trusts

Whereas Section 652 for simple trusts comprises about 300 words, Section 662 for complex trusts consists of approximately 700 words. Like Section 652, Section 662 carries the title statement:

Inclusion of Amounts in Gross Income of Beneficiaries of Trusts Accumulating Income or Distributing Corpus. The key differences here are the terms "accumulating income" and "distributing corpus." Otherwise, Section 662 has identical subsection headings to those of Section 652.

As to the key differences, subsection 662(a) reads that the inclusion—

Shall be . . . the sum of:

(1) Amounts required to be distributed currently . . . without the deduction for charitable purposes . . . [which] *includes any amount required to be paid out of income or corpus to the extent such amount is paid out of income for the taxable year,* [plus]
(2) All other amounts distributed . . . [where] *properly paid, credited, or required to be distributed . . . for the taxable year.* [Emphasis added.]

The subsection (a) goes on to say—

If the sum of [the above] *exceeds the distributable net income* [DNI] *. . . then, there shall be included in gross income . . . an amount which bears the same ratio to the* [DNI] *reduced by the amounts specified in (1) . . . as the other amounts in (2) bear to the other amounts property paid, credited, or required to be distributed to all beneficiaries.*

No question about it: this portion of subsection 662(a) is confusing. When interpreting this kind of statutory wording, it is helpful to think of Schedule K-1 as an assignment of a trust's *taxable income* only. Therefore, the DNI proration priority is on those amounts required to be distributed currently. If the DNI amount is not all used up, the "other amounts" then are proportionately assigned.

Another way is to think of a complex trust as a simple trust first, followed by an "other amounts" trust second. It is in this sense that a complex trust constitutes a "two-tier" taxation of beneficiaries.

Income required to be distributed currently falls into tier (1). The tier (2) amounts are those in excess of tier (1) to the extent that the distributable net income (DNI) exceeds the amounts in tier (1).

K-1 Income Assignments

If you look at an official K-1, you'll not find any grouping expressly headed **Income** . . . as you do on Form 1041. This means that you have to read the entry items in column (a) of the K-1 and compare them with the instructions in column (c), to digest what constitutes income to the beneficiaries. Doing this with the aid of Figure 10.2, we find as follows:

	Col. (a)	Col. (c)
I	Interest	Sch. B (1040), Part I
II	Dividends	Sch. B (1040), Part II
III	Capital gain	Sch. D (1040), short/long
IV	Annuities, businesses, & other nonpassive income	Sch. E (1040), Part III: Nonpassive
V	Rental real estate, royalties, & other passive income	Sch. E (1040), Part III: Passive

The column (a) income classes I, II, and III (interest, dividends, and capital gain) are quite straightforward. They are traditional portfolio income sources. They are pure investments of money and capital which require only minimal oversight by the trustee.

Class IV (annuities, businesses, etc.) comprises a special category of *nonpassive* income sources. They generally derive from the material participation activities of the trustor prior to his/her demise, and thereby retain the same income character in the trust. The term "other nonpassive income" includes any trade or business, any rental activity other than real estate, and any working interest in oil and gas properties that the trustor may have had.

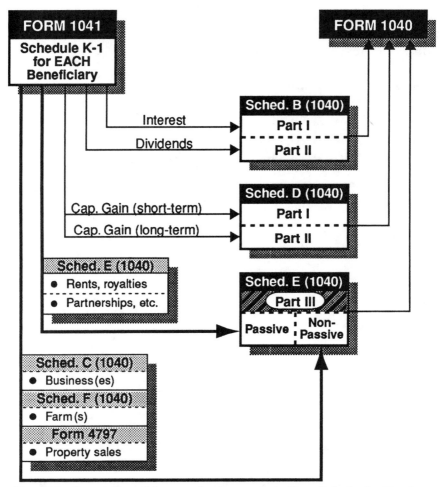

Fig. 10.2 - Correlation of Income Assignments to Beneficiaries by Trustee

Class V (rental real estate, etc.) comprises a separate grouping known as *passive activity* income sources. They are "passive" in the sense that capital investment in real property holdings or tangible property holdings constitutes the principal income-producing mechanism. Any personal services of the trustor (previously) or of the trustee (currently) are limited in terms of everyday supervision and control. As a consequence, special loss limitation rules apply to all passive activities, including partnerships and S corporations.

The tax law on passive activities (Class V above) is Section 469. This section is titled: *Passive Activity Losses and Credits Limited.* In essence, Section 469 limits the losses from one or more passive activities to the aggregate amount of positive income from all other passive activities. For example, if the positive net income from one passive activity is $5,000 and the net loss from another passive activity is <$17,500>, the net net loss of <$12,500> is disallowed for that year. Since losses cannot be passed through to the beneficiaries (except in the final trust year), Section 469 puts a damper on the type of activities engaged in by the trust.

Characterizing K-1 Income

The income portion of Form 1041 lists eight sources of gross income, as follows:

1.	Interest	5.	Rents, partnerships, etc.
2.	Dividends	6.	Farm income/loss
3.	Business income/loss	7.	Ordinary gain/loss
4.	Capital gain/loss	8.	Other income (identify)

These sources are passed through to Schedule K-1 where they are classified as:

I.	Interest	IV.	Nonpassive income
II.	Dividends	V.	Passive income
III.	Capital gain		

Except for classes I, II, and III, there is no one-to-one correlation between the gross income of the trust and the distributable net income (DNI) that appears on Schedule K-1. The K-1 rules require that the distributable income be characterized proportional to its origin in the trust. What do you do?

Suppose, for example, that the gross income (items 1 through 8 above) totals $12,000 on Form 1041. Of this amount, suppose the interest income is $3,000, dividends are $2,400, and the capital gain is $1,500 (subtotaling $6,900). Further, suppose that the distributable net income is $10,000 (after administrative deductions). What portion of this $10,000 DNI is characterized as interest, dividends, and capital gain?

The answer is as follows:

- Interest $= 10,000 \times \dfrac{3,000}{12,000} = 2,500$

- Dividends $= 10,000 \times \dfrac{2,400}{12,000} = 2,000$

- Cap. gain $= 10,000 \times \dfrac{1,500}{12,000} = \underline{1,250}$

$$5,750$$

This leaves $4,250 (10,000 – 5,750) of the DNI to be shared by Classes IV and V on the K-1. Of the five non-one-to-one items on Form 1041, which are Class IV (nonpassive) and which are Class V (passive)? You have a problem with this, don't you?

Material Participation: The Key

Referring to Form 1041, the K-1 classes IV and V derive from item 3 (Business income/loss), item 5 (Rents, partnerships, etc.), item 6 (Farm income/loss), item 7 (Ordinary gain/loss), and item 8 (Other income: identify). Your task as a trustee is to examine the origin character of all five of these items and segregate those which are nonpassive (material participation) from those which are passive (nonmaterial participation). Keep in mind that the term "origin character" means **in** the trust. Also, be mindful that the term "material participation" generally means 500 or more hours per year of personal time and attention, either by the trustor or trustee.

Section 469(h)(1) defines material participation as follows:

*A taxpayer shall be treated as materially participating in an activity **only if** the taxpayer **is involved** in the operation of the activity on a basis which is—*
(A) regular,
(B) continuous, and

(C) substantial. [Emphasis added.]

In the context of a trust, the term "taxpayer" refers to the trustor, the trustor's spouse, or the trustee, if the trustee separately engages in the activity distinctly apart from his general duties as a trustee.

The likely candidates for nonpassive (Class IV) income are Schedule C (1040): ***Profit or Loss From Business*** (item 3), Schedule F (1040): ***Profit or Loss From Farming*** (item 6), and Form 4797: ***Sales of Business Property*** (item 7). These are nonpassive in the trust ONLY IF transferred thereto directly from the trustor (or trustor's estate) who, while alive, did indeed materially participate in that activity.

Otherwise, every business-like activity of the trust constitutes passive income (Class V). This is particularly true of rental real estate, other rentals, royalties, partnerships, S corporations, other trusts, annuities, etc.

When in doubt as to whether a K-1 item is nonpassive (Class IV) or passive (Class V), always assume that it is *passive*. If the net income from an activity is positive, there is no pass-through tax distinction between its being passive or nonpassive. A distinction is made only in net loss situations (for each activity).

Deductions & Credits Limited

The official title of Schedule K-1 includes the term "Deductions, Credits, etc." Accordingly, you have to ask yourself: What are the actual deduction items and credit items that are preprinted on a K-1? Answering this, you'll find that they are limited in number and scope. They are limited because the primary purpose of the K-1 is to pass through taxable income **from** the trust **to** the beneficiaries. Any deductions and credits that pass through are of secondary importance.

Nevertheless, looking at a K-1, deductions and credits appear in five places as follows:

- Nonpassive income (Class IV)—
  before directly apportioned deductions

- Passive income (Class V)—
  before directly apportioned deductions

- Estate tax deduction

- Foreign taxes

- Deductions in final year of the trust

Note the two identical phrases: *before directly apportioned deductions*. What do these phrases mean? Each phrase on the K-1 is followed by separate line entries for—

a. Depreciation   _____
b. Depletion   _____
c. Amortization   _____

These items (depreciation, depletion, amortization) are called "cost recovery" or "return of capital" items. They represent the diminution of corpus to the extent applicable to each property held by the trust. Depreciation is a deduction allowance for the wear and tear of structures and equipment; depletion is a deduction allowance for the exhaustion of natural resources; amortization is a deduction allowance for the acquisition of intangible assets such as goodwill, covenants, customer lists, etc.

For simple trusts, the cost recovery (deduction) allowances seldom are apportioned to the beneficiaries. Most always, they are absorbed by the trust. This makes more actual cash available for distribution.

In a complex trust, there is need to accumulate income pursuant to the terms of the trust instrument. The accumulations may be intended for charitable contributions, generation skippings, college funds, major medical expenditures, long-term care of elderly beneficiaries, and so on. In such cases, the deduction allowances for depreciation, depletion, or amortization have to be allocated between that income retained by the trust, and that which is distributed currently to the beneficiaries. The allocation between the trust and beneficiaries is in direct proportion to the current income retained by the trust and that currently distributed to beneficiaries.

The *estate tax deduction*, when applicable, is usually only a one-time affair. It is a deduction for any estate tax paid by the trust, to the extent-equivalent of any allowed expenses which were unpaid at the time of the decedent trustor's "final return." This situation occurs when the trustee "takes over" operational affairs before the executor (of the estate) has completed his transitional tasks.

If the trust assets consist of share holdings in foreign-based corporations, a foreign tax is paid on the dividends earned abroad. There is "double taxation" on these dividends: by the U.S. **and** by the foreign nation. Because of this double taxation on the same income, a foreign tax credit may apply. This necessitates that each K-1 recipient prepare Form 1116: *Foreign Tax Credit*, and attach it to his individual Form 1040. The K-1 allocates in U.S. dollars the amount of foreign tax withheld from the dividends by each foreign jurisdiction.

A Simple Trust Example

Now that we've told you what goes on a K-1, let's give an example of how K-1s are most frequently used. For this purpose, consider a simple family trust. Assume that there are three beneficiaries whose designated allocable shares are A: 50%, B: 30%, and C: 20%. Also, assume that all administrative expense deductions are shared proportionately by all sources of trust income. Being a simple trust, there is no charitable deduction to be concerned about.

Many simple trusts have rental real estate as their primary income-producing asset. Such asset may consist of residential rentals, commercial rentals, industrial rentals, farmland rentals, or some combination thereof. Real estate, when properly managed, is durable and long lasting. It has the potential for appreciation when the trust is ready for termination.

With the above in mind, consider the following illustrative scenario of trust income and administrative expenses:

Interest	$ 1,000
Dividends	3,000
Capital gain	5,000
Net rents	36,000
Total income	45,000
Administrative expense	<5,000>
Net amount to be distributed	$40,000

What is the "proper way" to prepare each beneficiary's K-1? Is there a simpler way than the proper way?

The proper way is to go through the detailed allocation procedure that we outline for you in Figure 10.3. Believe us; we have used income and expense amounts in simple rounded numbers. Unround the numbers and increase the number of income sources and/or the number of beneficiaries. Then watch simplicity become complexity . . . computationally.

From our experience, when there are more than two beneficiaries of a trust, we use an "80% rule of thumb." That is, if the primary asset produces 80% or more of the total trust income (such as item 4 in Figure 10.3), we assign all income to that asset class. We do this for K-1 purposes only: NOT for Form 1041 purposes. This way, there is only one entry to be made on the K-1 for each beneficiary. The more the beneficiaries, and the more the K-1 entries for each, the more the K-1 information is misunderstood, misused, misreported, or not reported by the beneficiaries. Most beneficiaries understand that trust income — regardless of its origin character in the trust — is includible somewhere on their individual Form 1040 return. The most understood "somewhere" is the 1040 income line which reads:

Rental real estate, royalties, partnerships, S corporations, trusts, etc. Attach Schedule E.

The most understandable portion of Section E is its Part III titled: **Income or Loss From Estates or Trusts.** If any K-1 entries go elsewhere than on Schedule E, confusion and oversights mount.

STEP 1	Allocating the Character of Income			
	Class of Income	Amount	Allocation Fraction	Allocated Amount
1	Interest	$ 1,000	0.0222	$ 888
2	Dividends	3,000	0.0666	2,664
3	Cap. gain	5,000	0.1112	4,448
4	Net rents	36,000	0.800	32,000
	TOTALS	45,000	1.0000	40,000
	LESS All Administrative Deductions	< 5,000>	See Text	↑
	NET AMOUNT DISTRIBUTABLE	40,000		

XXXXXXXXXXXXXXXXXXXXXXXXXXXXXXXXXXXXXXXXXXXXXXXXXXXXX

STEP 2	Assignment to Designated Beneficiaries		
	Distributable Amount	A : 50%	B : 30%	C : 20%
1	888	444	266	178
2	2,664	1,332	800	532
3	4,448	2,224	1,334	890
4	32,000	16,000	9,600	6,400
	TOTALS	20,000	12,000	8,000

Fig. 10.3 - Worksheet for Allocating Currently Distributable Income

Other Simple K-1 Uses

The last category of items on Schedule K-1 is the grouping designated: *Other (itemize)*. There are eight entry lines here, (a) through (h). The first two have preprinted designations, namely (a) credit for prepaid taxes, and (b) tax-exempt interest. The other six are blank. Those designated (b) through (h) — seven in all — provide opportunities for distributing various forms of nontaxable money to the beneficiaries. A simple trust can use these lines, once all of its current (taxable) income is assigned to the beneficiaries who, in turn, report that income on Schedule E (1040), Part III.

Our position is that any trust whose total assets are $3,000,000 (3 million) or less should be structured as a simple trust only. Also, the trust should be structured to terminate in 25 years or less, without any accumulations of current income or any contributions to charity. A competent and responsible trustee can easily — and prudently — distribute $3,000,000 over a 25-year period. On average, that would be $120,000 per year (120,000/yr x 25 yrs = 3,000,000). Depending on the special needs of different beneficiaries, some years might distribute more; other years less. In reality, though, most "ordinary" trusts involve assets of considerably less than $3,000,000.

With the above in mind, let us postulate another scenario for using the K-1 in a simplified manner. The trust assets have been prudently managed, resulting in the following items being available for distribution:

(b)	Tax-exempt interest	$ 38,000
(c)	Depreciation reserve	30,000
(d)	Depletion reserve	20,000
(e)	Amortization reserve	10,000
(f)	Money market cash	25,000
(g)	Nontaxable annuity proceeds	15,000
(h)	Return of stock capital	12,000
		$150,000

When any of these items are distributed to beneficiaries, the allocable share distributable amounts are **not** taxable to the recipients. Yes, this statement is correct! Every beneficiary of a trust loves to receive nontaxable income.

Any distribution of tax-exempt interest (which also includes tax-exempt dividends) must be entered on the designated preprinted line (b) on the K-1. This is because any such amount must be diminished by its "allocable share" of direct costs and indirect expenses. As a trustee, your duty is to make sure that tax-exempt distributions be burdened with their share of the trust's operating expenses.

Taxable distributions bear their share of expenses; so, too, must the nontaxable distributions. When nontaxable distributions bear "their share" of operating expenses, it reduces the expense burden on the taxable distributions. The effect is that the taxable amounts are somewhat larger than they might otherwise be. And, correspondingly, the nontaxable amounts are somewhat smaller than they might otherwise be. Nevertheless, the overall procedural result is as depicted in Figure 10.4.

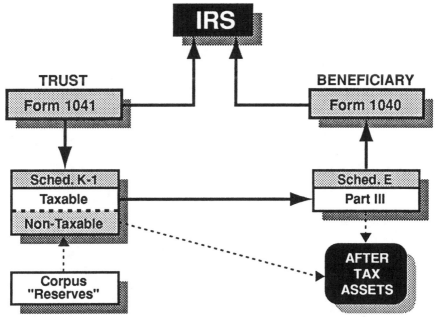

Fig. 10.4 - Two Single-Entry K-1 Items for Simple Trust Distribution

Complex Trusts & Charities

There is no way that a complex trust can accomplish the simplicity of the K-1 entries depicted in Figure 10.4. This is because a complex trust involves complex issues, set-asides, and distribution options. The complications arise strictly from the accumulations of income and distributions of corpus for special purposes, such as:

(1)   the attainment of a specified age by beneficiaries who are minors or young adults;

(2)   special care needs for disabled or elderly beneficiaries;

(3)   deaths of successive beneficiaries;

  (4) provisions for generation-skipping transfers; and
  (5) contributions to charity and charitable remainders.

Whereas a simple trust may display two or three taxable entries on a K-1, a complex trust may have five to seven such entries. These additional entries imply three things. One, greater trust assets, perhaps amounts of $3,000,000 or more. Two, greater discretionary options and management skills by the trustee. And, three, greater tax sophistication by the beneficiaries and/or by the preparers of their 1040 returns. Trusts created after April 30, 1989 with charitable remainder provisions are especially complex.

Having greater assets means the generation of greater dividends and capital gains, greater passive income from real estate holdings; greater participation in active business enterprises (including farming); and a greater desire to contribute to charity as a means of reducing income taxes on the trust for its accumulations and set-asides. (Recall Figure 10.2.) If the accumulations occur for several years or more, the trust taxation process — called *throwback taxation* — becomes unbelievably complex.

Many creators of complex trusts are fascinated with "charitable remainder" features. Charitable remainder trusts (called: CRTs) are exempt from tax on the accumulated earnings of the trust . . . PROVIDED that all remainder interests — both income and corpus — go exclusively to charity. Additionally, the life expectancy for which the charitable remainder interests are computed is based on no more than two living beneficiaries. The noncharitable beneficiary(ies) must receive no less than 5% of the trust assets annually . . . and be taxed on them. When the survivor deceases, what's left goes to charity. The trust, then, terminates.

11

TAX AND PAYMENTS

> If All Current Income Is Passed Through To Beneficiaries, No Trust Tax Applies. If So Much As One Taxable Dollar Is Retained, There Are Tax And Payments To Be Made. The "Total Tax" Is Computed On Schedule G (1041) Which Includes: (1) Regular Tax, (2) Capital Gain Tax, (3) Recapture Tax, (4) Alternative Minimum Tax, (5) Household Employment Tax . . . And Others. Various Credits May Apply To Reduce The Tax, The Most Important Of Which Is The "Foreign Tax Credit." If The Total Tax Of The Trust Is $1,000 Or More, ESTIMATED PREPAYMENTS Are Required.   For This Purpose, Voucher Forms 1041-ES Are Used.

Trusts are not tax avoidance conduits. This has been the message that we've tried to get across several times previously. Any income derived from the trust assets is taxed either at the trust level, at the beneficiary level, or at some point in between. This is clearly so implied from the official title of Form 1041: U.S. *Income Tax Return* for Estates and Trusts. If income is derived, it WILL BE taxed . . . somewhere in the process of its accounting, distribution, and consumption.

We are not concerned here with the tax computations and tax payments by the beneficiaries. Once taxable income has been passed through to them, and the trust takes its allowable "income distribution deduction" (as per Chapter 9), each beneficiary is on his or her own. While a trustee may be helpful to the beneficiaries in certain respects, he is not obligated to prepare and file each beneficiary's personal tax return. He is only obligated to prepare an allocably correct and timely filed Schedule K-1 (as per Chapter 10).

Otherwise, if there is any taxable income not passed through to the beneficiaries — for whatever reason — it must be taxed at the trust level. This is the purpose of the lower one-third portion of Form 1041. This portion is sectioned off and labeled: *Tax and Payments* (T & P). When there is tax computed by the trust, the trust pays that tax: not the beneficiaries.

The T & P section on the front page of Form 1041 starts off with *Taxable income*, and proceeds through to *Tax due* or *Amount overpaid*, as appropriate. We want to walk you through this portion of Form 1041 and its companion *Schedule G: Tax Computation*. As you'll see below, Schedule G (1041) has its own menu of taxes with its own association of schedules and forms.

Taxable Income Revisited

In the case of complex trusts, there invariably will be taxable income for which tax must be computed and paid. But, what about simple trusts? Are there situations where a trustee might opt to incur taxable income and pay the tax on it, rather than passing the tax burden through to the beneficiaries? Yes, there are such situations. But, first, a quick review of what constitutes the taxable income of a trust.

The taxable amount follows from the line entries on page 1 of Form 1041 which read:

☐	Adjusted total income (ATI)	$_____
(1)	Income distribution deduction (IDD)	_____
(2)	Estate tax deduction (very rare)	_____
(3)	Exemption amount ($300 simple; $100 complex)	_____
(4)	Total deductions. Add (1), (2), and (3)	<_____>
•	Taxable income. Subtract (4) from ATI	_____

As you can surmise from what we've said previously, the dominant deduction item is IDD. If the trustee claimed no such deduction or only a partial IDD, there would be taxable income to the trust. Are there any advantages to this? Yes, we think so.

Consider, for example, a simple trust with five beneficiaries. None of them is tax sophisticated, or maybe just one or two are. Issuing a taxable K-1 to them is meaningless; it can be confusing and intimidating. If the recipients were filers of 1040 EZs, 1040As, or basic 1040s, they would have to file an unfamiliar form, namely Schedule E (1040), and compute the tax in an unfamiliar manner. In this situation, wouldn't it be better for the trust to compute and pay the tax, then pass through after-tax (nontaxable) money to such beneficiaries? No K-1s need be furnished: just a transmittal letter with a check attached.

Or, the trustee could have sold a piece of rental real estate with substantial capital gains. The total tax would be one amount if the deal were all cash; it would be another amount if it were an installment sale over a 5- or 10-year period. As we'll show you in a numerical example later, the capital gains rate (15% as of 2004) starts lower down the taxable income threshold for trusts than it does for beneficiaries. The 15% rate starts at about $2,000 for trusts; at about $30,000 for single beneficiaries, and at about $60,000 for married beneficiaries. We have to use the term "around" because of year-to-year adjustments for inflation. Since the trust has to carry all of the operational, passive, and capital losses that it incurs, isn't it strategically better to absorb these losses with capital gains than to retain the losses until the trust terminates?

There is also a third reason why a simple trust may opt to pay the tax. Where there are uncertainties and ambiguities in the tax laws, the IRS loves to challenge transactional facts two or three years **after** events have taken place. It uses its audit powers to do so, with its merciless hindsight: called, "economic reality audits." It is better that such audits be conducted at the trust level, where a professional tax representative can be engaged. Most beneficiaries live in fear of an IRS audit, and are panicked by the thought of having to face one. A competent trustee can coordinate such matters quite effectively.

Thus, our position is that optional taxation of the trust is not all bad. There are times when it is simply better for the trust to pay the tax than for the beneficiaries to do so. We summarize our position in this respect in Figure 11.1.

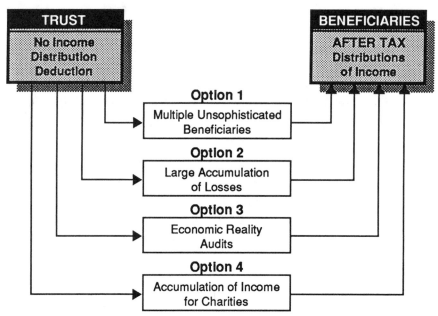

Fig. 11.1 - Benefits of Optional Taxation by Trust, Simple or Complex

Overview of Schedule G

All of the income tax computations for a trust are done on its Schedule G (**Form 1041**). Actually, this statement is not quite true. The computations are done on other schedules and forms, and are then summarized on Schedule G. In addition, various tax credits may apply. The abbreviated sequence of events is as follows:

- Regular taxes $ _____
- Applicable credits   < _____ >
- Other taxes   _____
- Total tax   _____

This sequence is officially displayed in a total of 13 entry lines on Schedule G. A highly abbreviated formatting of Schedule G is presented in Figure 11.2. It is advisable, of course, to always have an official Schedule G at your fingertips.

Sched. G (1041)	**Tax Computation**				*See Instructions*	
1	**Tax**					
		a	☐ Tax schedule ☐ Capital gain	a		
		b	Other taxes (list)	b		
		c	Subtotal - Add lines 1a & 1b	1c		
2	**Credits**					
		a	Foreign tax	a		
		b	Energy ☐ ☐	b		
		c	Business ☐ ☐ ☐	c		
		d	Prior min. tax	d		
3	**Total Credits.** Add lines 2a through 2d			3		
4	Tentative tax. Subtract line 3 from line 1c			4		
5	Recapture taxes ☐ ☐			5		
6	Alternative minimum tax			6		
7	Household employment tax			7		
8	Other taxes (list)			8		
9	**Total tax.** Add lines 4 through 8			9		

Fig. 11.2 - Edited Version of Schedule G (on page 2) of Form 1041

In Figure 11.2, note that the regular tax can be computed by one of two methods, namely:

☐ *Tax rate schedule*
☐ *Schedule D*: Capital gains & losses

These two checkboxes are followed by the line which reads: *Other taxes*. There are two such "other taxes." There is a 5-year/10-year averaging tax on lump-sum distributions to the trust from pensions and annuities of the trustor(s). There is a "Section 644" tax on property transferred to the trust at less than fair market value, then sold at a gain within two years of the initial transfer.

There are various tax credits that may apply to your trust. As indicated by the brackets (< >) above, a tax credit is a dollar-for-dollar offset against the regular tax. Four special credits and one general credit may apply. Probably the most important one for trusts is the Foreign Tax Credit: Form 1116. We'll amplify on this credit shortly.

In addition to regular (income) taxes, three other taxes may apply. These are—

- Recapture tax   Form 4255 or Form 8611
- Alternative minimum tax   Schedule I (Form 1041)
- Household employment tax   Schedule H (Form 1040)

The recapture tax applies to various credits which have been claimed, and where, subsequently, the property has been sold or the activity curtailed prior to the qualifying statutory period. The alternative minimum tax is a higher form of regular tax where certain tax preferences are claimed. The household employment tax applies to those trusts which pay $1,000 or more to domestic help for disabled or special needs beneficiaries.

Altogether, Schedule G (1041) covers up to 15 different taxes and credits. Obviously, we cannot discuss each and every one in meaningful detail. So, we'll pick and choose those which we believe are likely to be more common when administering trust property.

Capital Gains Example

Sooner or later, every trust with substantial capital assets will sell or exchange property which can produce capital gain. As we hinted at above, the capital gain tax is more favorable than the regular tax rate. Using 2004 as a reference year, the maximum capital gain rate was 15%. In contrast, the maximum regular tax rate was 35%. That's a 20% rate differential. Let's postulate a plausible example of how this maximum rate differential can be used advantageously by a trust (whether simple or complex).

Consider that your trust owns a multi-unit apartment building which generates net rental income of $35,000 for the year. You decide to sell the building. The net capital gain derived from the building amounts to $75,000. The trust has no other income. You report the sale on Form 4797: Sales of Business Property, which tells you to transfer the gain to Schedule D (Form **1041**), Part II: Assets Held More Than One Year. As you do so, you note Part V at the bottom of page 2 of Schedule D. It is captioned: *Tax Computation Using Maximum Capital Gains Rate.*

Let's compare the tax computations using both the regular rate and the capital gain rate. To keep matters simple, assume that there are no administrative deductions nor distributive deductions to be factored in. Thus, for our hypothetical example, the taxable income of the trust would be $110,000 ($35,000 ordinary income, plus $75,000 in capital gain). What would the regular tax be? What would the capital gain tax be?

Using the trust tax rate schedule for 2004, the regular tax would be $37,832. Correspondingly, the Schedule D, Part V tax would be $22,832. This is a federal tax saving of $15,000.

Better yet, suppose that the apartment building had several vacancies for several years, thereby accumulating $25,000 in passive losses. Additionally, the trust had accumulated $30,000 in capital losses from mutual fund redemptions over the years. These two losses total $55,000. None are distributable to the beneficiaries. There is no ordinary income for the year: just the capital gain of $75,000. How do the two tax computations compare now?

Using the 2004 rates again, the regular tax would be $5,200; the capital gain tax would be $3,000. There is not much difference here. However, when you compare these amounts with those above, there's a $20,000 to $30,000 tax reduction (22,832 − 3,000 = 19,832); (37,832 − 5,200 = 32,632).

Thus, obviously, when a trust has accumulated undistributable losses, and has the potential for generating capital gains, taxing the trust makes good sense.

Alternative Minimum Tax

What does not make sense is the alternative minimum tax which is computed on **Schedule I** (Form 1041). This is a cumbersome form, imposing a punitive tax. Schedule I is punishment for taking advantage of allowable options when establishing the trust's taxable income. The punishment is the "adding back" of some 25 tax preference items that initially reduced the trust amount taxable. The addbacks create a fictitious reference item called: Alternative Minimum Taxable Income (AMTI).

If the AMTI amount exceeds $22,500, the regular tax rate schedule and the capital gain rate go out the window. In their place is a flat 26% rate for AMTIs under $175,000; a flat 28% rate for AMTIs over $175,000. The whole AMT affair is a convoluted process vaguely explained in 5,000 words of official instructions (approximately the length of 14 pages of this text). The Schedule I alone comprises 62 lines of possible entries. Yes, 62!

Of the 25 addback items, only about six are likely to be applicable to trusts. This is because trusts tend to be more conservatively managed than ongoing business enterprises. The six most likely addbacks are:

(i)   Investment interest paid.
(ii)   State, local, and foreign income taxes paid.
(iii) Miscellaneous deductions exceeding 2% AGI.
(iv)   Depreciation allowances for real property.
(v)   Depletion allowances for mines, wells, natural deposits.
(vi)   Tax-exempt interest from private activity bonds.

Items (i), (ii), and (iii) are direct addbacks from page 1 of Form 1041. Item (iv) consists of all real property depreciation in excess of 40-year, straight line. Item (v) is all depletion in excess of cost basis depletion. Item (vi) is all tax-exempt interest and dividends from private activity bonds (sports stadiums, opera houses, etc.).

To arrive at the AMTI, you start with the adjusted total income on page 1 of Form 1041. To this amount, you *add* all of the applicable addbacks, then *subtract* an "adjusted" income distribution deduction (from Part II of Schedule I). Next, by following the preprinted instructions on Schedule I, you "phase out" the $22,500 exemption and apply the 26% or 28% flat rates as directed. This gives you a *tentative* minimum tax. If this tentative amount is greater than the regular tax **before credits**, the difference is the trust's AMT tax. If this AMT amount is large enough, it can wipe out most of the allowable credits, including the capital gains rate.

Foreign Tax Credit

If large enough, the AMT amount can wipe out all allowable credits that may have reduced the regular tax. This wipe-out includes any benefits from using the capital gains rate. The only credit that is salvageable is the foreign tax credit. This is fortunate because many trusts invest in international mutual funds and foreign exchange brokers. Without this credit, there would be "double taxation" on interest, dividends, rents, royalties, and other income derived from sources outside the U.S.

Enter, now, **Form 1116**: Foreign Tax Credit. This form, while not fully self-explanatory, is far easier to follow than Schedule I for AMT. The key to using Form 1116 advantageously is to sort out all foreign source income — country by country — that is subject to tax by the host country *and* by the U.S. Adjustments are made to the foreign source income for directly related and indirectly related expenses and losses. The result is the *net* foreign source taxable income (country by country). The amount of foreign income tax paid or accrued is expressly entered on Form 1116 . . . in U.S. dollars.

The gist of computing the U.S. credit for foreign taxes paid is as we depict in Figure 11.3. As you can see, the credit is based on the ratio of foreign taxable income to U.S. taxable income. The U.S. taxable income *includes* the foreign taxable income. We call this ratio the "FTR": Foreign Tax Ratio. The FTR is applied to the regular U.S. tax to determine the maximum amount of credit.

Caution is required for FTR purposes, if the regular U.S. tax was figured using the maximum capital gains rate. To figure the FTR, the U.S. taxable income is *reduced* by a 0.2929 fraction of the net capital gain of the trust. The 0.2929 fraction is the difference between the maximum regular rate (39.6%) and the 28% maximum capital rate, divided by 39.6% [(39.6 − 28) ÷ 39.6]. There is a special worksheet in the Form 1116 instructions that tells you how to refigure the FTR.

Suppose, for example, that the FTR turns out to be a 0.1515. And, suppose that the total foreign income taxes paid to all foreign countries is $2,000. Assume that the corresponding U.S. tax is

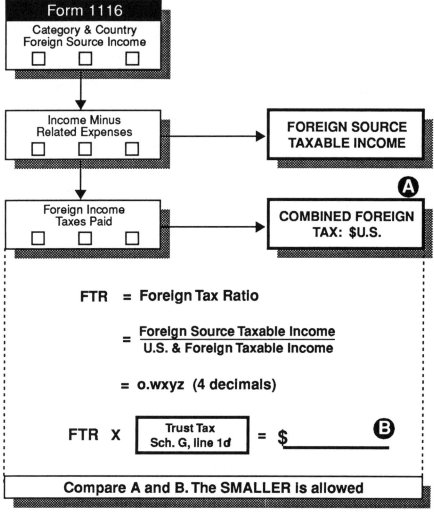

Fig. 11.3 - The "Key" to How the Foreign Tax Credit Works

$10,000 for Case A, and $15,000 for Case B. What is the foreign tax credit for Cases A and B?

Answer:

Case A — 0.1515 x $10,000 = $1,515

The rules say, "use the **smaller** of foreign tax or the credit tax."

Case B — 0.1515 x $15,000 = $2,273

Since the foreign tax is smaller than the credit tax, the current year credit is limited to $2,000. However, the unused $273 of the credit tax can be carried over to the following trust year.

Household Employment Tax

Most family trusts provide for the long-term medical and special-needs care of elderly, senile, and disabled beneficiaries. To administer this care, there is need to employ domestic help for such tasks as caretaking, nursing, housecleaning, cooking, gardening, driving, and so on. Such hired help is classed as "household employees" (if age 18 or over).

If the trust pays **any one** household employee cash wages of $1,000 or more in a given year, a new set of trustee duties emerges. The term "cash wages" means payments by cash, check, or money order, and reimbursement for commuting expenses in excess of $65 per month. The term does not include the value of any food, lodging, clothing, or other noncash items given to the domestic worker. The $1,000 or more rule applies to any two or more workers engaged in a calendar quarter.

First off, the trustee has to see that each household worker has a valid social security number (SSN) or other tax identification number (TIN). For each such worker, a Form W-2: Wage and Tax Statement, has to be prepared by the trustee. In addition, the trustee has to impose and collect (a) social security taxes, (b) medicare taxes, (c) federal unemployment taxes, (d) income tax withholdings (if requested by the worker), and (e) credit the worker for earned income less than $28,000 per year.

To compute, hold, and pay over to the IRS the above taxes, **Schedule H (1040):** *Household Employment Taxes* is used. This schedule has 28 entry lines and eight sets of Yes-No questions. This schedule and its five pages of instructions (about 5,000 words) are quite self-explanatory. However, figuring the federal unemployment tax (FUTA) requires a knowledge of the state unemployment tax rules where the workers work. You can run into extensive frustration here. In the end, though, the bottom line on

Schedule H (1040) transfers to the next to bottom line on Schedule G (1041). The Schedule H tax combines with all other taxes and credits that enter on Schedule G for the trust.

Accumulations for Charities

As we touched on back in Chapter 8: Administrative Deductions, a trust can contribute to charity and get a current year's tax deduction for it. Either income, or corpus, or both, can be contributed. Further, if a complex trust, the income can be accumulated for distribution in subsequent years. This is the gist of Code Section 642(c)(1): *Deduction for Amounts Paid for a Charitable Purpose; General Rule.* A "charitable purpose" is addressed in depth in Section 170(c): *Charitable Contribution Defined.*

When a contribution is made or an amount is accumulated for charitable purposes, **Form 1041-A** is required. This form is titled: *U.S. Information Return; Trust Accumulation of Charitable Amounts; For calendar year* _____. The 1041-A is arranged in four parts, of which Part II is the most revealing. It is subtitled: *Distributions of Income Set Aside for Charitable Purposes.*

Particularly note the wording in the title of Form 1041-A. The form is an *information return*; it is not a tax return. No tax amount is computed on it.

As an information return, Form 1041-A is to bring to the IRS's attention the precise dollar amount and specific charitable purpose of each year's charitable deduction(s). In complex and "high flyer" trusts, the alleged charity is often a reverent sounding disguise by which private individuals and entities enjoy the benefits of tax-exempt income. It is for this reason that at every line on Form 1041-A where a charitable deduction amount is claimed, a preprinted instruction reads—

Itemize by charitable purpose; include payee's name and address.

The instructions which supplement Form 1041-A add:

Do not merely enter the category (i.e., religious, charitable, scientific, literary, or educational), but also enter the purpose of the deduction. For example, "payment of $4,000 to indigent persons for medical purposes," or a "grant of $25,000 to equip the chemistry lab at the University of _____."

Figure 11.4 displays this instruction in more succinct form. As you can see, the first entry line summarizes the prior accumulations for which a deduction was claimed. The next five lines are itemizing each and every current year distribution. The balance and current-year set asides are carried over to the following year. The message in Figure 11.4 is that there must be *continuous accounting* for all charitable deductions ever claimed.

The IRS is very serious about Form 1041-A. Pursuant to Section 6652(c)(2), it is authorized to assess a penalty of $10 per day, up to a maximum of $5,000 against both the trust **and** the trustee for not filing Form 1041-A on time. Additional penalties apply if the information provided is false or misleading.

Payments with Extensions

Unless a trust distributes currently *all* of its adjusted total income, there will be a trust tax to pay. It is the total tax from Schedule G, after credits, that is transferred to page 1 of Form 1041. The transfer is directed to the line identified as—

Total tax (from Schedule G).

Next follow several lines identified as **Payments**, ending with the line *Total payments.* The clear implication is that if there is a total tax, there must be total payments. The payments are required even if the trustee files application(s) for extensions of time to file the 1041 return (with all of its attachments). The extension requests apply only to filing deadlines: not to payment deadlines. This point is frequently missed by many trustees.

Some trustees, and many beneficiaries, too, develop what we characterize as the "extension syndrome." They file for extensions of time year after year . . . after year. They do this because the

Form 1041-A	U.S. INFORMATION RETURN		Current Year
XXXXXXXXXXXXXXXXXXXXXXXXXXXXXXXXXXXXXXXXXX			
Part II	Distribution of Income Set Aside for Charitable Purposes		
1	Accumulated income set aside in prior years for deductions claimed under Sec. 642(c)	1	
2	Income set aside in prior years for which a deduction was claimed **and** which was distributed during current year.		
	a — Enter by — a		
	b — "charitable purpose" — b		
	c — Include each — c		
	d — payee's — d		
	e — name & address — e		
3	Total current year's distribution ▶	3	
4	Cumulative balance. Subtract 3 from 1	4	
5	income set aside during current year (for which a deduction was claimed)	5	
6	Carryover to following year. Add 4 and 5	6	

Fig. 11.4 - Use of Form 1041-A: Trust Accumulation of Charitable Amounts

agony getting the accounting affairs of the trust together and filing on time numbs their senses and disorients them. Filing on time is a matter of self-discipline and attention to duties. Repeated extensions of time make it difficult for the beneficaries to file their own 1040 returns on time.

There are valid reasons for requesting an extension of time to file. Among these are illness, injury, out of town, out of country, disaster (fire, flood, earthquake, hurricane), missing information, erroneous information, undue hardship, and so on. When any of these reasons exist, there are two IRS forms that the trustee can use. The first is a 3-month *automatic* extension of time (Form 8736): no reason need be given. The second is an additional 3-month extension (Form 8800), but ONLY IF there is an *adequate explanation*.

Extension Form 8736 shows a "balance due" line. Instructions on this form say you MUST pay the full estimated balance due, even if the 1041 (plus attachments) is filed three to six months later.

Estimated Payment Vouchers

If the total tax for the trust is $1,000 or more, special *prepayment* procedures apply. These procedures require the use of **Form 1041-ES**: *Estimated Income Tax for Estates and Trusts*. This form is used throughout the taxable year. Our position is that instead of relying on extensions of time to file, and making rash payments at that time, make payments in advance throughout the year. This gives you "coasting time." Use this time to prudently prepare Form 1041 and its schedules on or before the regular annual due date. Making regular scheduled prepayments of estimated taxes is an insurance policy against penalties and other unexpected events.

Form 1041-ES consists of four payment vouchers, each preprinted and dated as follows:

Voucher No.	Due Date
1	April 15
	(2 months)
2	June 15
	(3 months)
3	September 15
	(4 months)
4	January 15

Note that these are NOT quarterly payments of tax due; they are *estimated* prepayments of an amount of tax not yet known and due. The 4th payment is in mid-January. This is after the close of the calendar year prior to January.

An instruction on each voucher reads:

File only if the trust is making payment of estimated tax. Return this voucher with check or money order payable to "United

States Treasury." Write the trust's EIN and "Form 1041-ES" on the check or money order. Do not send cash.

Instructions that accompany Form 1041-ES provide a 17-step worksheet for figuring the estimated tax with a fair degree of accuracy. But it's another form to fill out, and another record to keep. Our approach is to simply make an educated guess at the likely taxable income of the trust. Use the prior year's trust tax as a starting point. Increase it or decrease it as you surmise the income to be. Apply a 40% tax rate; divide the result by 4; then "round up" to an even $500 amount.

For example, suppose the estimated taxable income is expected to be "around" $22,000. At 40%, the estimated tax would be $8,800. Dividing this by 4 comes to $2,200. Round this amount up to $2,500 per payment voucher. Make the voucher payments on time, then experience vanishing preoccupation with tax penalties and interest.

When doing the actual return, should you find that you have overpaid, the overpayment can either be refunded, or it can be credited to the following year's estimated tax. The very last two tax and payment lines on Form 1041 accommodate your wishes in this regard.

12

TERMINATING THE TRUST

A Trust Terminates When There Is A HAPPENING OF AN EVENT By Which The Duration Of Distributions Is Measured. Upon Notice To The Remainderpersons, Complete Liquidation Of The Corpus Income-Producing Assets Is Generally Required. This "Winding Down" Often Produces Capital Losses And Other Deductions And Expenses Which Exceed Gross Income. If So, IRC Section 642(h) — The "Final Year Loss" Rule — Becomes Useful. Taxation Relief Is Signified By Checking The Box "Final" On Form 1041 AND On Schedule(s) K-1. In Contentious Cases, Petitioning For Release From Duty Is Prudent.

At some point after its creation, every trust must terminate. Ideally, this is determined by reference to some specified event taking place with respect to one or more of the beneficiaries. A typical such event, for example, would be the death of the surviving trustor, or, the youngest child of the trustor reaching a specified age. In other words, there must be **some event** by which the duration of the trust can be measured. Once the terminating event is identified — and its happening confirmed — the trust must terminate. A reasonable time for doing so is allowed.

So emphatic is the termination aspect that most states, today, have enacted probate laws against perpetuities. Most rely on the *Uniform Statutory Rule Against Perpetuities*. The essence of this uniform rule is that a trust shall terminate—

At the expiration of a period of time not exceeding 21 years after the death of the survivor of specified lives in being at the creation of the trust or other property arrangement. [CPC ¶ 21209 where CPC is "California Probate Code."]

Thus, a trust provision which expressly states or implies that it may not be terminated is ineffective.

On termination, the trustee continues to have the powers reasonably necessary under the circumstances to wind up the affairs of the trust. The "winding up" is what this chapter is all about. This means a final distribution of the property, or a liquidation of all assets and the complete distribution of proceeds. The final distributee is either the trust-designated remainderman, or a court-designated legatee, or both. There is also a final accounting to be made, a final tax return to be filed, and one or more final Schedules K-1 to be prepared.

Ordinarily, a trustee is automatically released from his duties when all trust records are closed. However, in some cases it is more prudent to seek official release through the probate court, the IRS, and state taxing agencies. Terminating a trust is a separate process of its own. There are serious trustee duties to be performed.

Identify "The Event"

The first place to look for identifying the terminating event is the trust instrument itself. If you followed our suggestion back in Chapter 4 about "dissecting the contract" (Figure 4.1, Item XIX), you'll know instantly where to start looking. You first look for the after-death paragraphs sprinkled throughout the trust. Then you look for the contingency paragraphs. These matters are not too difficult to identify in simple trusts.

The following is an actual example of how an after-death termination clause may read:

Upon the death of the surviving trustor, the principal and any accumulated income of the trust estate shall be distributed to—

A. The trustor's first son,   ___(Name)___

B. The trustor's daughter,   __(Name)__
C. The trustor's second son,   __(Name)__
D. The trustor's grandson,   __(Name)__
E. The trustor's granddaughter,   __(Name)__

Following each distributee's name, there is assignment of a dollar amount and/or fractional interest in one or more property items. Then follows a contingency clause, such as—

If [A, B, C, D, or E] *does not survive the trustor, that deceased distributee's share shall be distributed in accordance with subparagraph F hereof.*

From here on, the termination instructions get fuzzy. Even in a simple trust, termination contingencies are imposed. Here's a good example:

If any beneficiary entitled to outright distribution of the trust estate or a portion thereof is under age 25, the trustee shall hold and administer the beneficiary's portion of the trust estate for his or her benefit . . . until said beneficiary attains the age of 25. If a beneficiary dies before attaining age 25, the property retained for him or her shall be distributed to the beneficiary's issue, or if there is none, to the trustor's then living issue by right of representation. However, if the deceased beneficiary is a grandchild of the trustor, his or her share shall instead be distributed to his or her estate.

Are you beginning to get the idea that what might appear initially as a clear termination event falls prey to obfuscation clauses designed to keep the trust alive for as long as possible? The termination event is made even more cloudy in complex trusts, charitable remainder trusts, and generation skipping trusts.

In reality, it is always difficult to find a clear and irrefutable termination clause in a trust. The most likely reason is the ambivalence of the legal profession and the reluctance of custodial financial institutions to part with the property of a trust. A lot of hidden and costly fees are coveted by nonbeneficial interests who don't want to let go until the assets are milked low. It takes an astute and brave trustee to counter these covetous interests.

What Probate Law Says

As illustrated above, rarely does a trust instrument provide a clear direction as to when and how the trust shall terminate. The more designated beneficiaries there are, the more hopeless termination becomes. Augmenting this hopelessness is the fact that rarely is the word "termination" ever used in a trust instrument. This leaves you, as trustee, no choice but to review — and rely on — the trust law of the state having probate jurisdiction over the trust. The particular section of the probate code that you want to look for is titled: *Modification and Termination of Trusts* . . . or similarly titled.

For example, the California Probate Code (CPC), Section 15407: *Termination of Trust*, reads—

A trust terminates when any of the following occurs:

    (1)   The term of the trust expires.
    (2)   The trust purpose is fulfilled.
    (3)   The trust purpose becomes unlawful.
    (4)   The trust purpose becomes impossible to fulfill.
    (5)   The trust is revoked.

Of the items listed, the most powerful for termination logic is that the purpose of the trust has been fulfilled or that its purpose is becoming increasingly impractical to fulfill. Using this logic, if some clear event or circumstance in the trust instrument signifies the creator's intent to start dissolving the trust, its primary purpose would seem to have been served. This means rereading the purpose and intent of the initial trustor and formulating his or her intentions into practical events of accomplishment. In this respect, the trustee has the advantage of hindsight, which a trustor does not. The beneficiaries themselves also have the advantage of hindsight. As we depict in Figure 12.1, all of this hindsight starts the process of thinking about other factors for terminating the trust.

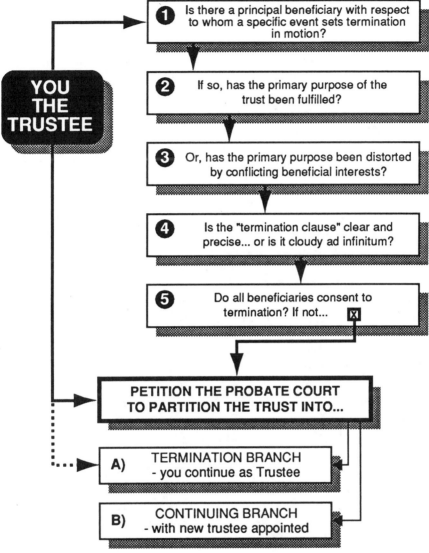

Fig. 12.1 - Factors to Consider When Terminating a Trust

As to the advantage of hindsight, CPC ¶ 15404 is instructive. This probate law section enables the living beneficiaries to **compel** termination of the trust. The instructive wording is—

(a) If all beneficiaries of a trust consent, they may compel termination of the trust.

*(b) If any beneficiary does not [so] consent . . ., the other beneficiaries, with the consent of the [probate] court, may compel a **partial termination** of the trust if the interests of the beneficiaries who do not consent are not substantially impaired.* [Emphasis added.]

Our position is that once the primary purpose of the trust has been served, the practical approach is to at least partially terminate the trust. Once this is accomplished, then request the appointment of a new trustee to administer the interests of the nonconsenting beneficiary(ies). Quite often, nonconsenting beneficiaries tend to be those who regard a trust as a tax sheltering arrangement, rather than as a distributive sharing contract. They want to manipulate the trust in the hopes of making millions of dollars and paying no tax. Let some other trustee take on that responsibility. You bow out when you can. A condensation of our position in this regard is the A-B branching portions of Figure 12.1.

What the IRS Says

On the issue of when and how to terminate a trust, IRS Regulation 1.641(b)–3(b): *Termination of trusts*, is instructive. This subregulation reads essentially in full as—

*The determination of whether a trust has terminated depends upon whether the property held in trust **has been distributed to the persons entitled** to succeed to the property upon termination of the trust rather than upon the technicality of whether or not the trustee has rendered his final accounting. A trust does not automatically terminate upon the happening of the event by which the duration of the trust is measured. A reasonable time is permitted after such event for the trustee to perform the duties necessary to complete the administration of the trust. . . . Further, a trust will be considered as terminated **when all the assets have been distributed except** for a reasonable amount* *which is set aside in good faith for the payment of unascertained or contingent liabilities and expenses.* [Emphasis added.]

The gist of the above seems to be that the trustee can set the termination process in motion, once he has identified—

the happening of the event by which the duration of the trust is measured.

Obviously, the triggering event must be confirmed with certainty. This means studying and interpreting the wording in the trust agreement and, if necessary, obtaining a written professional opinion on the event-happening. If a trust professional is hesitant to confirm your interpretation of the event-happening, pay the costs and seek a ruling from the probate court of jurisdiction.

Once the event-happening has been confirmed by an independent source other than your own, you can start distributing the corpus and income to the remaining beneficiaries. You have a reasonable time to prepare and complete the distribution process. How long is "reasonable time"? There is no statutory answer. A year or two, or three, would be appropriate for properly winding up the affairs of a trust that has been in operation for 10 years or so. A trustee can use his own common sense and judgment on this. Just don't unduly prolong the process.

Notify the Beneficiaries

You have no obligation to consult with beneficiaries as to whether the termination event has occurred or not. Once the event is confirmed by a trust professional or by the probate court, your responsibility is to notify all remainderpersons (successor beneficiaries) of your intention to terminate. Cite the event, and make reference to the appropriate wording in the trust instrument. Invite comments and expressions of preferences as to the property items a beneficiary would be willing to take.

Summarize the property items remaining in the corpus, and cite their approximate total value. Tell each beneficiary the exact percentage of his distributive share of the residual estate. Make sure that all individual percentages add to 100%. You want to make clear that the entire residual estate will be distributed as promptly as possible. Inform the remainderpersons that there will be contingency holdbacks for taxes, debts, expenses, and fees.

The problem with most trusts is that, when termination time comes, the bulk of the income-producing assets are illiquid. The principal illiquids are real estate holdings, operational businesses and farms, partnerships and S-corporation interests, trust deed notes, and other securities that are not readily marketable. Any hasty liquidation of these items may prompt charges of impropriety or imprudence on your part.

If any of the remainderpersons are willing to take the property in lieu of cash, you need to establish what their proposed titling arrangement would be. We can pretty much assure you that when there are three or more remaining beneficiaries, there will not be unanimity as to what property to take and what title form to take it in. Invariably, some beneficiaries will want to sell, while others will want to hold on to it. As a trustee, you have no obligation to arbitrate any property-taking disagreements among the beneficiaries.

We know of a case where the predominant property holding was a $3,000,000 (3 million) shopping mall in a small town. The property generated about $200,000 a year in gross income. The trust had been in operation for about 10 years when the termination event occurred. The successor beneficiaries were four siblings: three brothers and one sister. The oldest brother and the sister were financially well off and did not want to terminate the trust. The second oldest brother wanted out . . . now. The youngest brother also wanted out, but he worked as a partner in the oldest brother's business. The second oldest brother sued the trust for his $750,000 distributive share ($3,000,000 ÷ 4). He won. The property had to be refinanced to pay off the plaintiff brother. Some seven years later, the youngest brother was still trying to cash out his $750,000 distributive share.

The lesson in the above case is simple. As a trustee, when you notify the successor beneficiaries of your intention to terminate, anticipate nonagreement. Inform the ultimate distributees that if no agreement is reached within 90 days as to how the property is to be taken by them, you will list the property for sale with a reputable broker. If one or more distributees want to stop the sale, let them sue. They will have to do so under trust law provisions, such as CPC ¶ 17200 – ¶ 17211: *Judicial Proceedings Concerning Internal Affairs of Trust; petition by trustee or beneficiary.*

All costs of such litigation are borne by the trust. As a result, the beneficiaries lose . . . but their attorneys win. Many a trust has been depleted prematurely by prolonged and senseless litigation. When the assets are reduced to $20,000 or less, the trustee has the absolute power to terminate the trust without anyone's consent [CPC ¶ 15408(b)].

Accounting for Liquidation Proceeds

It's an age-old problem: liquidating trust assets in order to make final distribution of the corpus and income equitably. Clearly, the trustee has the power and duty to do so. Yet, over the years there has been much litigation against the trust and trustee during the liquidation process. It takes a tough minded trustee to weather the allegations and complaints by hostile beneficiaries and their attorneys. Probate law is on the trustee's side so long as title to the property is vested in the trust. Tax law is also on the trustee's side.

Often, estate sales result in significant capital losses. Who gets to claim the losses for tax purposes: the trust or the residuary legatees? The "residuary legatees" are the remainderpersons for the final distributive years of a trust.

The answer to this question was set forth by the IRS in a Special Ruling dated as far back as August 16, 1950 [505 CCH ¶ 6180]. This ruling reads in part that—

Where trust assets were sold, upon liquidation of the trust following the death of the life tenant, and the proceeds distributed to the remaindermen, the gains and losses realized in such transactions were to be included on the fiduciary return filed for the trust.

This ruling was challenged by numerous legatees and remaindermen (remainder*persons*: the preferred term today). All these persons wanted to take the capital losses on their own personal

1040 returns. In 1953, the U.S. Supreme Court [in *Anderson v. Wilson*, 3 USTC ¶ 1066, 289 US 20, 53 SCt 417] ruled that—

No loss was deductible by the residuary legatees upon distribution to them of the proceeds of sale of property sold by the trust at a loss.

Other similar cases and rulings followed, to wit:

Under state (Nebraska) law, capital losses realized by a trust were chargeable against the trust corpus. Therefore, the taxpayer, an income beneficiary, was not entitled to deduct losses resulting from the trust's disposition of corporate stock and commodity futures. [*C.W. Swingle*, 18 TCM 594, Dec. 23,673(M), TC Memo 1959-135.]

Losses from the sales of securities made by a trustee in order to distribute the corpus of a trust to 50 remaindermen after the death of the life beneficiary were not losses of the remaindermen. [*Coachman*, 16 TC 1432, Dec. 18,385.]

What is the practical effect of these cases?

There are two answers. One, in the termination years **before** the final/final Form 1041 and Schedules K-1 are filed, the trust is administered as a simple trust. This means that once the termination event has incurred, there are no more accumulations and set asides, regardless of what the trust instrument says. This also means that all net current income, including capital gains, are passed through allocably to the income remainderpersons. Any net capital losses due to liquidation are assigned to the residual corpus principal which is passed through, nontaxably, to the distributees.

The second answer to the above question is that all *carryover* losses are retained by the trust: operating losses, capital losses, and passive losses. These losses are retained by the trust until the *final/final* year of the trust accounting. In that final year — and only in that year — all residual losses which are unusable by the trust are then passed through to the remainderpersons. This is the only practical accounting way to "close the books" on the trust.

The "Final Year Loss" Rule

Before closing the trust, we need to tell you about IRC Section 642(h). This tax code section is titled: *Unused Loss Carryovers and Excess Deduction on Termination Available to Beneficiaries.* It reads in pertinent part as follows:

If on the termination of a trust, the trust has—

> *(1) a net operating loss carryover . . . or a capital loss carryover . . ., or*

> *(2) for the last taxable year of the trust deductions . . . in excess of gross income for such year,*

then such carryover or such excess shall be allowed as a deduction, in accordance with regulations prescribed by the [IRS], to the beneficiaries succeeding to the property of the trust.

We call Section 642(h) the "final year loss" rule. As we've stated several times previously, losses, ordinarily, do not pass through each year to the beneficiaries. They are retained in the trust to be used for accounting offsets from year to year. If, in the last taxable year of the trust, there are remaining unused losses, they are then passed through to the succeeding beneficiaries.

If you'll examine the above cited provisions closely, you will note that there are three kinds of loss pass-throughs. They are:

1. Net operating loss,
2. Capital loss, and
3. Excess deductions.

A net operating loss is an ordinary (operational) loss where the deductions for a given year exceed the operating income. A capital loss is a transactional loss (involving the sale or exchange of corpus assets) for a given year in excess of $3,000. An excess deduction appears only in the final year of a trust. It is computed independently of any net operating loss or capital loss carryovers.

One statutory clause was intentionally omitted from subsection 642(h)(2) above, regarding excess deductions. That clause reads—

Other than the deductions allowed under subsection (b) [relating to personal exemption] *and subsection (c)* [relating to charitable contributions].

Our reading of this is that in the very last taxable year of the trust, there is no allowance of a trust exemption [$300 simple; $100 complex] and no allowance for any charitable contributions. This makes sense. The primary purpose of the trust has been served; therefore, the trustee is obligated to wind down affairs rather than keeping the operation going.

There is another practical point to be noted. In the final year, there will invariably be more expenses and deductions than income. This is because the primary income-producing assets have been liquidated, and the proceeds stored in either (a) noninterest bearing accounts, (b) low interest bearing accounts, or (c) tax-exempt interest bearing accounts. At this stage, maximum income is not the focus: liquidity is.

We summarize in Figure 12.2 the final year focus of a trustee. There are definitely more accounting activities in the last taxable year of a trust than at any other time. The applicable IRS regulations thereon should convince you of this fact.

Excerpts from Regulations

There are approximately 3,500 words of IRS regulations governing the interpretation of Section 642(h). There are five such regulations, captioned as follows:

1.642(h)-1: *Unused loss carryovers on termination of a trust.*
1.642(h)-2: *Excess deductions on termination of a trust.*
1.642(h)-3: *Meaning of "beneficiaries succeeding to the property of the trust."*

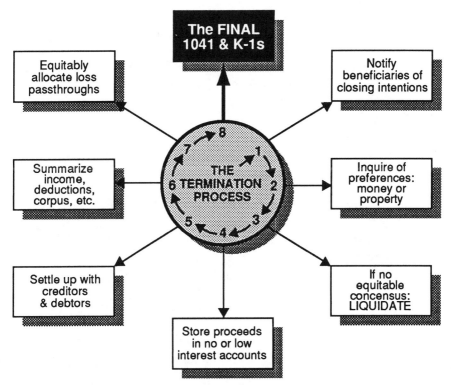

Fig. 12.2 - Your Focus of Duties When Terminating a Trust

1.642(h)-4: *Allocation among the beneficiaries.*
1.642(h)-5: *Comprehensive example.*

For instructional purposes, we'll interpret the gist of these regulations, and cite an excerpt or two, where pertinent. Otherwise, you can access these regulations on your own, or engage a tax professional to do so for you.

The gist of Reg. (h)-1 is that the character of the losses in the trust, when passed through to the beneficiaries, maintains the same character. This includes separating the net operating loss into two forms (a) for regular tax purposes, and (b) for minimum tax purposes. This also means segmenting the capital loss into (a) short-term and (b) long-term elements.

The gist of Reg. (h)-2 is that the net operating loss carryover and the excess deduction amount allowed cannot be duplicative. That is,

*A deduction based upon a net operating loss carryover will
never be allowed to beneficiaries under both paragraphs (1)
and (2) of section 642(h). . . . However, if the last taxable year
of the trust is the last year in which a deduction on account of a
net operating loss may be taken, the deduction, to the extent not
absorbed in that taxable year by the trust, is considered an
"excess deduction" under section 642(h)(2).*

The gist of Reg. (h)-3 is expressed best through its
subparagraph 3(d), to wit:

*A remainderman who receives all or a fractional share of the
property of the trust as a result of the final termination of the
trust is a "beneficiary succeeding to the property of the trust."
For example, if property is transferred to pay the income to A
for life and then to pay $10,000 to B and distribute the balance
of the trust corpus to C, C and **not** B is considered to be the
succeeding beneficiary.* [However], *if the trust corpus is
insufficient to pay B his full $10,000 then B would be the
succeeding beneficiary.* [C would receive nothing; he, therefore,
would not be a succeeding beneficiary.]

The gist of Reg. (h)-4 is that the carryovers and excess
deductions are allocated among the succeeding beneficiaries in
proportion to the share of each in the burden of the loss or
deductions.

The comprehensive example in Reg. (h)-5 is too involved for
discussion here. We can do better by translating the regulatory
example (about 850 words and figures) into the entry lines on the
final Schedule K-1.

The Final K-1

The final Schedule K-1 for each succeeding beneficiary is where
all of the distributive action lies. You signify your intention in this
regard by checking the box in the upper right-hand corner of the
schedule. This checkbox appears as—

☒ *Final K-1*

While checking this box, reread the title of Schedule K-1: [Each] *Beneficiary's Share of Income, Deductions, Credits, etc.*

Keep in mind that you are engaged in a "winding down" process. In all likelihood, therefore, there will be nil positive income entries on the K-1. The bulk of the entries will be deduction items in the section captioned: *Deductions in the final year of the trust.* We list all of the applicable line entries for the final year, in Figure 12.3. We show this caption as line number 12. [The "12" signifies coordination with the 12th and final chapter of this book.]

Sched. K-1 (Form 1041)	Beneficiary's Share of Income, Deductions, Credits, etc.		☒ Final K-1	
Beneficiary's Tax ID		Trust's Tax ID		
XXXXXXXXXXXXXXXXXXXXXXXXXXXXXXXXXXXXXXXXXXXX				
(a) Allocable Share Item		(b) Amount	(c) Enter on Form 1040	
12	Deductions in final year	/////////	/////////	
a	Excess deductions	< >	Sched.A: Misc.	
b	Short-term capital loss	< >	Sched.D: S/T	
c	Long-term capital loss	< >	Sched.D: L/T	
d	Net operating loss, regular	< >	Form 1040: Other	
e	NOL for minimum tax purposes		Form 6251	
f				
g				
IMPORTANT NOTE: There is no allocable sharing of any charitable deduction unusable by the trust				

Fig. 12.3 - Final Year Deductions That Pass Through to Remainderpersons

Back to Regulation 1.642(h)-5 above. It sets up the following numerical example:

Taxable interest	$2,500
Business income	3,000
Gross income	$5,500

Business expenses	$5,000
Administrative expenses	9,800
Total deductions	$14,800

There is also an unused capital loss of $5,000. In this regulation, the IRS is using low-value numbers. This makes it easier to identify the basic procedures involved.

When total deductions exceed gross income, as in the example above, the first step is to determine the net operating loss amount. To do this, you have to adjust the total deductions for those not attributable to business income. As such, the numbers are:

Deductions before adjustment	<$14,800>
Adjustments: 9,800 – 2,500	7,300
Deductions after adjustment	< 7,500>
Gross income	5,500
Net operating loss carryover	<$ 2,000>

The <2,000> amount is entered in the K-1 at the line designated as 12d in Figure 12.3. Even though the line caption uses the word "loss," we prefer placing brackets < > around the entered amount. This emphasizes that it is a negative number and, clearly, a *deduction* by the distributee. Where there is more than one final distributee, the deduction amount has to be allocated between them.

The "excess deductions" are those which are not taken into account when computing the net operating loss. This is the $7,300 figure in the tabulation above. Accordingly, <7,300> is entered on the K-1 at the line designated as 12a in Figure 12.3.

The net operating loss deduction does not include any capital losses whatsoever. Therefore, the $5,000 capital loss postulated for the IRS example has to be segmented into its short-term and long-term components. The result could be <2,000> entered on line 12b, and <3,000> on line 12c in Figure 12.3.

Line 12e, net operating loss for minimum tax purposes, is line 12d (for regular tax purposes) adjusted for any tax preferences which were used when tallying up the business expenses for the year. The net effect is to decrease the amount of loss entered at line 12e. The less this particular loss, the better it is for the beneficiaries.

Note also in Figure 12.3 that there are two blank lines: 12f and 12g. These are for other final year deduction items. One such item could be any unused passive losses from rental real estate activities. Another such item could be any unused general business credits.

The Final 1041

There is a single, central idea behind the final year deductions on Schedule K-1. It is to clear out from the trust everything possible that can be passed through to the beneficiaries, for their own income tax returns. Since these passthroughs are loss-type, they are useful in offsetting other positive sources of income by each beneficiary.

Because of the income-sheltering effect of the final passthrough, you, as trustee, must make sure that the Form 1041 backup accounting is rock solid. You want to assemble all of the backup schedules and attachments that you can. This extra accounting effort alone almost assures that the last taxable year of the trust will be an NOL year (NOL is Net Operating Loss). As such, there would be no taxable income passed through to the beneficiaries. There would be no taxable income to the trust, either.

To make sure that the trust's NOL computation is correct, you must procure **Schedule A (Form 1045)** and its instructions. This schedule is titled: ***Net Operating Loss Computation***. The first applicable entry line on Form 1045, Schedule A is—

Trusts, enter taxable income   <_____>

The "taxable income" must be a **negative** amount. It would be, where the total deductions exceeded the gross income of the trust.

Using figures in the previous IRS example, the taxable income would be <$9,300>. [$5,500 gross income minus $14,800 total deductions.] There follow thereafter some 20 items of *Adjustments* on Schedule A (1045), before arriving at a NOL figure that is assignable to the beneficiaries. You'll need to read the Form 1045 instructions carefully, to do the "adjustments" correctly.

Another attachment to Form 1041 that you need to be careful about is Schedule D (1041), Part IV. This portion of Schedule D

(Capital Gains and Losses) is titled: *Capital Loss Carryovers*. It is arranged into three sections, namely:

A — Carryover Limit
B — Short-Term Capital Loss Carryover
C — Long-Term Capital Loss Carryover

The first line entry in Section A is—

Enter taxable income or (loss) from Form 1041.

In the IRS example on the preceding page, the startoff entry amount would be <9,300> .

Subsequent procedures are preprinted directly on a *Capital Loss Carryover Worksheet* (14 lines) in the general instructions to Form 1041. Instructions at the last entry line in Sections B and C read:

If this is the final return of the trust, enter on Schedule K-1 (Form 1041), at line _____ [12b for short-term; 12c for long-term].

If the trust operated a business or farming activity, various tax incentive credits (15 in all) may have been applicable. If so, any unused credits can be "reformulated" and passed through to the beneficiaries. For this purpose, Form 3800: *General Business Credit* is used.

Another potentially applicable attachment is Form 8582: *Passive Activity Loss Limitations*. This is applicable to rental real estate and trust participation in partnerships, S corporations, estates, and other trusts where the deductions have exceeded the incomes therefrom. The excess of aggregate deductions over aggregate income is called: *unallowed passive losses*. In the final year of the trust, however, these "unallowables" can be distributed, allocably, to the remainderpersons.

Any passive losses that pass through to the remainderpersons are not automatically allowable to the recipients. Each remainderperson on his or her own Form 1040 must comply separately with the loss limitation rules of Section 469.

Keep a Contingency Reserve

How do you signify to the IRS that this, indeed, is the last taxable year of the trust? It is a "taxable year" even though, in actuality, no final tax may be due (by the trust). You signify your intent by checking that little box in the headportion of Form 1041 which reads—

☒ *Final return*

This is the only notice that you need to give the IRS that the activities of the trust are about to terminate. The IRS's internal computer processing then takes over.

To the IRS, what does the term "Final return" mean? Keep in mind that we are addressing Form 1041. This is an **income** tax return; it is **not** a corpus tax return. This distinction is important, particularly when winding down the affairs of the trust.

Consequently, checking the box *Final return* means three things to the IRS. The meanings are that:

1. No further tax accountable income is being generated by the trust . . . nor will there be. Amounts of less than $600 are not considered tax accountable.

2. No further deduction or credits will be passed through to the remainderpersons.

3. Some residual corpus liquidity remains to be distributed. The IRS is not computer concerned about this because any such residual distributions are not further tax accountable. Such amounts were transfer taxed when the corpus and principal were initially assigned to the trust.

Thus, filing a final Form 1041 does not mean — nor should it mean — that all corpus liquidity has been 100% disbursed and distributed. Common sense and prudence require that you retain a certain dollar amount on hand for contingencies. Inevitably, there will be some.

Examples of the need for contingency funds to defray closing expenses are:

(a) Collection, organizing, and librarying of records for successor interests.

(b) Summarizing, by distributee, all K-1 distributive sharing from "Day 1."

(c) Summarizing, by distributee, all prior invasion, assignments, and distributions of corpus.

(d) Reviewing all prior and closing correspondence for any pending issues outstanding, such as litigation in process or threats of litigation by hostile beneficiaries and their attorneys.

(e) Closing out *all* bank, financial, creditor, debtor, and investment accounts . . . except one. Retain only one account. Make it a checking-only type (no interest) preferably. Keep your final days simple.

(f) And — yes — standby for a final IRS audit of the trust's books.

Certainly, you should distribute all corpus liquidity except for a reasonable amount to defray expenses for the final wrap-up. How much is a reasonable amount for retention?

Our estimate is somewhere between $10,000 and $30,000, depending on your experience in the activities of the trust. In any business relationship where money and people are involved, there are always emergencies and unforeseens. This is life. Therefore, you **must** keep some amount of corpus money on hand . . . until the very end.

ABOUT
THE AUTHOR

Holmes F. Crouch

Born on a small farm in southern Maryland, Holmes was graduated from the U.S. Coast Guard Academy with a Bachelor's Degree in Marine Engineering. While serving on active duty, he wrote many technical articles on maritime matters. After attaining the rank of Lieutenant Commander, he resigned to pursue a career as a nuclear engineer.

Continuing his education, he earned a Master's Degree in Nuclear Engineering from the University of California. He also authored two books on nuclear propulsion. As a result of the tax write-offs associated with writing these books, the IRS audited his returns. The IRS's handling of the audit procedure so annoyed Holmes that he undertook to become as knowledgeable as possible regarding tax procedures. He became a licensed private Tax Practitioner by passing an examination administered by the IRS. Having attained this credential, he started his own tax preparation and counseling business in 1972.

In the early years of his tax practice, he was a regular talk-show guest on San Francisco's KGO Radio responding to hundreds of phone-in tax questions from listeners. He was a much sought-after guest speaker at many business seminars and taxpayer meetings. He also provided counseling on special tax problems, such as divorce matters, property exchanges, timber harvesting, mining ventures, animal breeding, independent contractors, selling businesses, and offices-at-home. Over the past 25 years, he has prepared nearly 10,000 tax returns for individuals, estates, trusts, and small businesses (in partnership and corporate form).

During the tax season of January through April, he prepares returns in a unique manner. During a single meeting, he completes the return . . . *on the spot!* The client leaves with his return signed, sealed, and in a stamped envelope. His unique approach to preparing returns and his personal interest in his clients' tax affairs have honed his professional proficiency. His expertise extends through itemized deductions, computer-matching of income sources, capital gains and losses, business expenses and cost of goods, residential rental expenses, limited and general partnership activities, closely-held corporations, to family farms and ranches.

He remembers spending 12 straight hours completing a doctor's complex return. The next year, the doctor, having moved away, utilized a large accounting firm to prepare his return. Their accountant was so impressed by the manner in which the prior return was prepared that he recommended the doctor travel the 500 miles each year to have Holmes continue doing it.

He recalls preparing a return for an unemployed welder, for which he charged no fee. Two years later the welder came back and had his return prepared. He paid the regular fee . . . and then added a $300 tip.

During the off season, he represents clients at IRS audits and appeals. In one case a shoe salesman's audit was scheduled to last three hours. However, after examining Holmes' documentation it was concluded in 15 minutes with "no change" to his return. In another instance he went to an audit of a custom jeweler that the IRS dragged out for more than six hours. But, supported by Holmes' documentation, the client's return was accepted by the IRS with "no change."

Then there was the audit of a language translator that lasted two full days. The auditor scrutinized more than $1.25 million in gross receipts, all direct costs, and operating expenses. Even though all expensed items were documented and verified, the auditor decided that more than $23,000 of expenses ought to be listed as capital items for depreciation instead. If this had been enforced it would have resulted in a significant additional amount of tax. Holmes strongly disagreed and after many hours explanation got the amount reduced by more than 60% on behalf of his client.

He has dealt extensively with gift, death and trust tax returns. These preparations have involved him in the tax aspects of wills, estate planning, trustee duties, probate, marital and charitable bequests, gift and death exemptions, and property titling.

Although not an attorney, he prepares Petitions to the U.S. Tax Court for clients. He details the IRS errors and taxpayer facts by citing pertinent sections of tax law and regulations. In a recent case involving an attorney's ex-spouse, the IRS asserted a tax deficiency of $155,000. On behalf of his client, he petitioned the Tax Court and within six months the IRS conceded the case.

Over the years, Holmes has observed that the IRS is not the industrious, impartial, and competent federal agency that its official public imaging would have us believe.

He found that, at times, under the slightest pretext, the IRS has interpreted against a taxpayer in order to assess maximum penalties, and may even delay pending matters so as to increase interest due on additional taxes. He has confronted the IRS in his own behalf on five separate occasions, going before the U.S. Claims Court, U.S. District Court, and U.S. Tax Court. These were court actions that tested specific sections of the Internal Revenue Code which he found ambiguous, inequitable, and abusively interpreted by the IRS.

Disturbed by the conduct of the IRS and by the general lack of tax knowledge by most individuals, he began an innovative series of taxpayer-oriented Federal tax guides. To fulfill this need, he undertook the writing of a series of guidebooks that provide in-depth knowledge on one tax subject at a time. He focuses on subjects that plague taxpayers all throughout the year. Hence, his formulation of the "Allyear" Tax Guide series.

The author is indebted to his wife, Irma Jean, and daughter, Barbara MacRae, for the word processing and computer graphics that turn his experiences into the reality of these publications. Holmes welcomes comments, questions, and suggestions from his readers. He can be contacted in California at (408) 867-2628, or by writing to the publisher's address.

ALLYEAR Tax Guides
by Holmes F. Crouch

Series 100 - INDIVIDUALS AND FAMILIES

BEING SELF-EMPLOYED .... T/G 101
DEDUCTING JOB EXPENSES .... T/G 102
FAMILY TAX STRATEGIES .... T/G 103
RESOLVING DIVORCE ISSUES .... T/G 104
CITIZENS WORKING ABROAD .... T/G 105

Series 200 - INVESTORS AND BUSINESSES

INVESTOR GAINS & LOSSES .... T/G 201
PROFITS, TAXES, & LLCs .... T/G 202
STARTING YOUR BUSINESS .... T/G 203
MAKING PARTNERSHIPS WORK .... T/G 204
SMALL C & S CORPORATIONS........................... T/G 205

Series 300 - RETIREES AND ESTATES

DECISIONS WHEN RETIRING .... T/G 301
LIVING WILLS & TRUSTS.................................... T/G 302
SIMPLIFYING YOUR ESTATE .... T/G 303
YOUR EXECUTOR DUTIES .... T/G 304
YOUR TRUSTEE DUTIES .... T/G 305

Series 400 - OWNERS AND SELLERS

RENTAL REAL ESTATE .... T/G 401
TAX-DEFERRED EXCHANGES   .... T/G 402
FAMILY TRUSTS & TRUSTORS.......................... T/G 403
SELLING YOUR HOME(S) .... T/G 404
SELLING YOUR BUSINESS .... T/G 405

Series 500 - AUDITS AND APPEALS

KEEPING GOOD RECORDS .... T/G 501
WINNING YOUR AUDIT....................................... T/G 502
DISAGREEING WITH THE IRS .... T/G 503
CONTESTING IRS PENALTIES .... T/G 504
GOING INTO TAX COURT .... T/G 505

For information about the above titles, contact
Holmes F. Crouch

Allyear Tax Guides

Phone: (408) 867-2628   Fax: (408) 867-6466